The Game for a Lifetime

More Lessons and Teachings

Harvey Penick

with Bud Shrake

A FIRESIDE BOOK
Published by Simon & Schuster

FIRESIDE
Rockefeller Center
1230 Avenue of the Americas
New York, NY 10020

First Fireside Edition, 1999

FIRESIDE and colophon are registered trademarks
of Simon & Schuster Inc.
Manufactured in the United States of America

10   9   8   7   6   5

Library of Congress Cataloging-in-Publication Data
is available.

ISBN 0-684-80059-4
ISBN 0-684-86735-4 (Pbk)

For Helen

Contents

Foreword

THIS IS THE book Harvey Penick was preparing when he fell ill with pneumonia in the spring of 1995. He passed away with Tom Kite at his bedside on a Sunday afternoon one week before Ben Crenshaw won a second Masters Championship in what seemed a supernatural manner, as if the spirit of his mentor had entered his mind and heart to guide him to this triumph.

Only two weeks earlier, again on a Sunday afternoon, Harvey had given the final lesson of his more than seventy years as a teaching pro. From his death bed, the ninety-year-old Penick spoke hoarsely as Crenshaw stroked balls on the carpet, using a hickory shafted Sarazen putter that was kept in the corner for lessons to pilgrims who came to the house seeking aid.

Ben placed his hands on the old putter, and Harvey began reminding Crenshaw of the boyhood stroke they had known together, a silky touch that has made Ben one of the finest putters in the history of the game.

"Trust yourself. Believe in yourself," the old master said.

When it was time for Ben to take his wife, Julie, and their two daughters home so Harvey could try to rest, the pupil leaned forward and kissed the master on the forehead and said, "I love you, Harvey."

"I love you, too, Ben. I'll be watching you always."

Ben swallowed hard, and his eyes misted. "I know you will," Ben said.

As he turned to leave the bedroom for what they knew would be the last time, there was a look on Ben's face as if an electric shock had struck his soul.

During the following week, Harvey had brief periods when he could breathe without the oxygen tube in his nose, and the pain in his back diminished, and he talked of returning soon to the practice range. He was excited at the prospect of giving lessons to country music legend Willie Nelson. Willie had signed "You Saved My Game" on the brim of a cap that Harvey wore.

Harvey urged visitors to look at his Willie cap and also at what had come in the mail—an Indiana University basketball autographed "To A Great Teacher," and signed "Bob Knight."

"I think I can help Willie," Harvey would say with a smile. "I hope it's not too late. I don't mean too late for Willie's game. I mean too late for me in general."

During those good periods, Harvey would bring up the new book he had been concentrating his efforts toward. He could no longer write legibly, though he continued to turn out pages until near the end. Every visit, no matter if he felt better or bad, he asked if I was certain his notes and letters were in a safe place.

He had given me three shoeboxes of papers and had urged me to dig through the larger boxes in the garage and through the folders in his briefcase, where among other treasures I found the attested scorecard from 1985 when University of Texas women's golf coach Susan Watkins, at that time an assistant pro at Austin Country Club, shot a women's record 73 from the men's Gold championship tees at the club's new Pete Dye course. The scorecard had been lost in Harvey's briefcase for a decade.

His final book, Harvey said, was for what he called seasoned players. By seasoned, Harvey meant golfers who had played the game earnestly for no telling how many years. He believed you could be seasoned at fifteen or at ninety-five, depending on the intensity of your experience with the game.

Harvey's purpose in making his final book was to entertain and enlighten seasoned players, reveal to them his beliefs, and encourage them to continue their romance with the most mysterious, most cerebral, most frustrating and supremely satisfying of all games that can be played by one person alone.

One morning on the practice range at Austin Country Club, months before pneumonia invaded him, Harvey had laughed when I repeated a remark I had heard from Waxo Green, the late Nashville sportswriter. Waxo had said, "You know you're getting old when all your irons start going the same distance."

Harvey nodded and grinned. Later, I saw him writing a note called "Waxo's Puzzle." In the next few days he started scribbling in notebooks and on scraps of paper.

Some pages were memories of experiences he'd had with friends and pupils. Some were a few sentences that told Harvey's points of view on playing golf, on learning the lessons of the game, on keeping in mind the joys and benefits of it in the face of the despair it can cause. He had been reminded of stories about club members and other golf pupils, including professionals, that always involved an instructional point and usually a smile. He felt that the heart of his teaching—Take Dead Aim—had not been fully understood by some, and he added to the explanation he had given in his *Little Red Book*.

His shoeboxes became stuffed with notes on and letters from seasoned players from all over the world with handicaps from less than zero to more than 30, with a range in age of about eighty years. He read the letters with a magnifying glass.

Harvey meant this book for those who have advanced into the mysteries of the game and may find his words helpful in understanding their obsession.

Harvey wrote his last note on Friday, March 3, after lecturing to an audience of amateurs, mostly high handicappers, who had gathered to hear him at the Golfsmith teaching academy that bears his name in north Austin.

His young nurse would huddle close beside him during these lectures and translate the questions from the audience for him. Harvey could barely hear. His hearing aids squealed. But he could understand the nurse's voice and was good at reading lips. Harvey loved these sessions. He said seeing the people laughing at his jokes and stories made him feel like Bob Hope or Jimmy Demaret.

That Friday evening the congestion in Harvey's lungs grew severe and the EMS was called to take him to St. David's Hospital, where his wife, Helen, had worked as a volunteer for many years.

On a stretcher in the ambulance, Harvey peered up into the eyes of a young paramedic. Harvey had never seen him before, but he recognized a seasoned player.

"You're a golfer, aren't you, son?" Harvey wheezed.

"Yes, sir." The paramedic hesitated. This might not seem like the right time. But, then again, when might he ever have another chance like this?

"Mr. Penick, would you please check my grip?"

Harvey gladly did so, for teaching was his joy. He pronounced it a good grip and told the paramedic to use it without fear and enjoy his game.

Then he beckoned the young man to bend close because Harvey's voice was growing faint.

"Remember to leave my share of your winnings in the pro shop," Harvey said. He smiled. That was a little joke he used with pupils for decades. He didn't expect anyone to do it, and they understood.

After seven days in the hospital, Harvey was sent home to die. He needed nurses around the clock. On his first day after returning to the house he shared with Helen on Fawn Creek Path, Harvey sat for a while in his wheelchair in the sunlight on the rear deck where he could see flowers and birds and squirrels and sense the water running over rocks in the creek bed below. He autographed a few of the hundreds of books that were stacked up and waiting. He read some of his mail. His strength began failing, and he asked to be put to bed where he lay for the rest of his life.

For the next three weeks, the Penick home was open to a stream of visitors. Harvey was always cordial, despite his illness. But he was growing weaker and more frail. In his prime, Harvey weighed 135 pounds. Now he had wasted down to 84. One morning when I entered his bedroom, Harvey was writing in a notebook. Seeing me, he shook his head. "I can't do it anymore," he said. He showed me the notebook. The page was covered with circles and scrawls. "I know what I'm trying to say, but this pen won't say it."

I thought Harvey was going to pass over on the Sunday that Ben and Julie Crenshaw and their daughters came to see him. Harvey had been trying to talk to me, but his breath was rasping and his lips refused to form words. When I met Ben at the front door, I said, "You'd better hurry."

A few minutes later, I was surprised to see Harvey roll over on one elbow and hear him loudly and distinctly say, "Go get the putter," to begin the last lesson with Ben.

Harvey fought off death several times in the next week. He was exhausted and in terrible pain, but he was determined to be at Austin Country Club on Sunday, April 2, for the unveiling of a bronze statue of Harvey and Tom Kite.

When sculptor Don Davis asked his permission, Harvey replied, "I've never done anything to deserve me being made into a statue."

Davis then asked Kite, U.S. Open Champion and at that time golf's all-time leading money winner. Kite answered, "I've never done anything to deserve me being made into a statue beside Mr. Penick."

By Saturday night, Harvey realized he would not be able to endure the journey of a few blocks from home to the club. He was clinging to life purely by willpower. He told friends who had gathered around him that he wanted the unveiling to be an occasion of celebration, not of mourning.

On Sunday afternoon, a musical ensemble played for a crowd on the lawn beside the clubhouse. The wrapping was removed from the statues. Revealed were two standing figures—Harvey as mentor studying the swing of pupil Kite. The teacher and the pupil gaze through the oaks down toward the first tee and the river.

In a sometimes trembling voice, Kite told the crowd, "When I am asked what is the biggest break I ever had in golf, I say it is when the IRS transferred my dad from the Dallas office to Austin. Because I arrived in Austin at age thirteen to encounter Mr. Penick and Ben Crenshaw. In my wildest dreams, I couldn't have hoped for a finer teacher or stronger competition."

The moment the ceremony ended, I went back to Harvey's bedroom with his lawyer, Richard Pappas, and we described the event. Harvey raised up as nearly as he could and grasped my hand with both of his and said, "I'm going to die now. I'm ready."

Kite came in a short while later. He had lingered at the club to be gracious to the crowd, as Harvey would have wanted. Tom sat and held his old teacher's hand and told him about the unveiling. Harvey asked how

Davis Love III was doing at the tournament at that moment in New Orleans. The late Davis Love, Jr., himself a great teacher, had been one of Harvey's favorite pupils on the University of Texas golf team and had played in the Masters as an amateur. Now the son needed to win in New Orleans to get an invitation to the Masters the next week.

Tom went into the living room, where family and friends were watching on the large color TV. Kite returned and told Harvey that Davis was in a playoff for the title in New Orleans. Harvey smiled and lifted his thin arms up to his face and clapped his palms together three times.

Shortly past five o'clock, Harvey's son-in-law, Billy Powell, entered the bedroom with the news that Davis Love III had won the tournament in New Orleans and qualified for the Masters. Sometime in these seconds, Harvey's soul passed on to somewhere else. "But I know Mr. Penick knows Davis won. I'm sure of it," Tom said at once.

Using his cellular phone out on the Penicks' deck above the creek, Kite called Crenshaw, who was having dinner in Augusta. It was the call Ben had been dreading. The two champions, both of them as bound to their teacher as sons to a father, made a plan. Kite would go to Augusta on Monday morning. He and Crenshaw would play practice rounds Monday and Tuesday. On Wednesday morning they would charter a plane to fly back to Austin to be pallbearers at Harvey's funeral.

Ben hadn't been playing well. He had missed the cut in a tournament, which is how he could be at the Penick house on the Sunday of the putting lesson two weeks before that final round at the Masters.

While Ben was hitting practice balls at Augusta National and making himself accept that he would soon be carrying Harvey's coffin, caddie Carl Jackson, who always handles Ben's bag at Augusta, spoke up to him, "Why don't you move the ball back a little in your stance, and then make a tighter turn with your shoulders."

Ben tried Jackson's suggestion. In just a few swings, Ben began hitting the ball as solidly as he had ever hit it. His confidence returned, and his youthful, graceful, classic swing along with it.

At a surprise party in Austin to celebrate Crenshaw's second Masters championship, both of them won with Carl Jackson on his bag, I asked the tall, thoughtful Jackson why it had occurred to him to offer Ben the advice that he did.

"I don't know exactly," he said. "I was watching him closely, and the words just suddenly were revealed in my mind what I must say to him."

It rained hard on the morning of the funeral, but the private plane from Augusta flew through the storms carrying Ben and Julie Crenshaw, Tom and Christy Kite, Terry Jastrow, the ABC-TV golf producer who had once become Texas Junior Golf Champ under Harvey's guidance, and Chuck Cook, the prominent golf teacher. Harvey's admirers packed the funeral home, many standing outside under umbrellas to be part of the service.

At the cemetery, Kite and Crenshaw, tears running down their cheeks amid the raindrops, helped to place their mentor's coffin in the shelter of the tent that protected the grave. Each of them laid a flower on top of the casket and bowed his head.

The sun came out as the Augusta party flew back that afternoon. On the following morning, Ben began his march toward the Masters title that captured the emotions of millions who watched it actually happen. It was an event that made sport universal, timeless and important. It was a parable of fathers and sons, of learning and teaching, of love and trial and inspiration and revelation, and perhaps a glimpse beyond the curtain.

During the final nine holes at Augusta on Sunday, the emotional tension grew thicker than the smell of southern pines and magnolias. Ben had said he was going to win the Masters for Harvey. Television and newspapers had played major stories linking Ben with the spirit of his mentor.

On everyone's mind was the awed question: Can this really be happening? When an errant shot by Crenshaw hit a tree but bounced into the fairway, a TV commentator said, "I bet Harvey Penick kicked that ball back in."

With Davis Love III tied for the lead up in front of him, Crenshaw hit a 6-iron as well as one can be struck at number sixteen, the seventieth hole of the tournament, then made a tricky, heart-stopping putt for a birdie. On the seventeenth green, Ben stroked a wide breaking putt across the slick grass into the cup for another birdie and a two-stroke lead over Love. At that point, Ben had needed only nine putts for the last eight holes. Remarkably, in four rounds he would not three-putt even one of Augusta National's greens, all of which are famously fast and deceptive.

After he holed out at the seventy-second hole for a one-shot victory, Ben bent and buried his face in his fingers for a moment, and then he lunged into the embrace of Carl Jackson and wept on the chest of the man who had carried his bag, and who had been inspired to reveal a few crucial words of advice at exactly the right moment.

All over the country people were watching that drama at the Masters on television and weeping with the sheer thrill of it, and everywhere people were thinking, Yeah, I do believe in angels.

Ben told the press, "I could definitely feel him with

me. I had a fifteenth club in my bag. The club was Harvey." After the Masters, Ben wrote a letter to Tinsley Penick that said, ". . . it gives me great pleasure to know that what your father tried to tell his pupils works not only today but for the rest of one's life."

It went largely unremarked in the excitement and wonder of Ben's second Masters, but in 1984 Ben had consulted Harvey for guidance before leaving for Augusta and had followed by winning his first Masters Championship in an enormously popular and sentimental victory.

In his introduction for Harvey's *Little Red Book,* which was published two months before Tom Kite won the 1992 U.S. Open at Pebble Beach, Crenshaw wrote that in many ways Harvey reminded him of the fabulous Scotsman Old Tom Morris, the philosopher from St. Andrews. Old Tom, Ben wrote, lived a fulfilling life knowing he contributed to others' enjoyment of the game.

Ben wrote: "Old Tom was wise, treated all men equally, and kept things very simple. It did not take much to make him happy. As long as he was around his many friends, and there was golf to be played and talked about, he was truly *contented*. Many times Old Tom would say 'I've got mae God and mae gowff to see me thro.' "

Harvey might well have said that, too, but in his Texas drawl. These are his last words on golf and on life.

—*Bud Shrake*
Austin, Texas, 1996

The Dreamer Sees the Real Thing

A FELLOW DROVE into the parking lot of our Pete Dye course beside the river. He parked his Mercedes-Benz with California plates in the shade of our live oak trees and walked into the golf shop and asked to see my son Tinsley, the head pro.

This visitor was a good-looking man with an athletic build. His clothes were top quality. His shoes were shined. His face glowed with health. Tinsley invited him into the grill room so they could have a glass of iced tea at a comfortable table while he waited to hear what the man wanted.

"When I was a kid, I was a terrific player," began his story. "Junior championships, state high school champ, played for a university team that did well in the nationals. Got married my senior year. I wanted to try the pro tour, but instead I started in sales for my father-in-law's company and made more money playing golf with clients my first year than any rookie on the pro tour made grinding his heart out.

"I've kept my game in good shape. My handicap is a traveling 4. In the last year, I've had a 68 at the Old Course, a 70 at Pebble Beach, a 70 at Pine Valley, for example, and there was one great day when I shot a 67 at Riviera. For a CEO who has made more money than he knows what to do with, and also has a handsome wife and family, I can really play golf."

Tinsley congratulated him on his success.

"But I'm not satisfied," the fellow said.

"Why not?" Tinsley asked.

"I still want to play on the pro tour."

Tinsley drank his tea and waited.

"This is no pipedream," the fellow said. "I'm talking about the Senior Tour. I'm forty-three years old. I have sold my company for a very large sum. I'm free now to do whatever I want. My plan is to move my family here and buy a house beside your golf course.

"Every morning for the next seven years I will show up on your doorstep, rain or shine. I want daily lessons from you, and I'd like your father to check me every week or so. I'll hit five hundred practice balls a day. I'll play golf every day from the tips on this very tough course. Soon as I reach the age of fifty, I'll turn pro and join the Senior Tour. I'll pay you and your father whatever you ask, if you'll agree to get me ready. What do you say?"

Tinsley didn't need long to think it over.

"Let me tell you about one of our club members," Tinsley said. "Like you, he's forty-three years old, and he's made all the money he'll ever need. He has a handsome wife and family. He practices golf every day, and he plays golf nearly every day. He's getting ready for the Senior Tour in seven more years. At this tough golf course, his handicap is a plus-4. He is your competition. He is the player you are going to have to learn to beat if you are going to go on the Senior Tour. I really don't want to spend seven years of my life trying to help you to do that. Not for any price.

"There's the man I'm talking about—he's sitting over by the window, eating a club sandwich."

Tinsley gestured toward Tom Kite.

What a Good Grip Can Do for You

JIM MANNING, THE golf coach at South Park High School, came to see me in the spring of 1952. Jim had been one of my players at the University of Texas, and it was good to visit with him again.

With him Jim brought a boy named Ed Turley, who had finished third in the state high school tournament at Memorial Park in Houston. Ed had come in behind two very good players from Houston—John Garrett, later a star for Rice, and Kirby Attwell, who never lost a Southwest Conference match after he joined our team at Texas.

Jim walked down the steps into my pro shop in the basement. He and the Turley boy had played a round that morning at the old Austin Lions Muny, the best golf course in town in those years, and Jim wanted me to go up to the range and watch his pupil hit a few balls.

Problem was, rain had begun falling.

Instead of going out in the rain, I handed young Turley a club and said, "Let me see your grip."

The boy placed his hands on the club as his father and Jim Manning had taught him, both V's pointing toward his right shoulder. His hands looked melted to the club. A good grip has obvious class, like the hands of a concert pianist. It gives me pleasure to see a good grip.

I said, "Anyone with a grip like that is either a good

player now, or he will be by the time he leaves the University of Texas. I'm going to ask our Athletic Director, D. X. Bible, to let you live in the athletic dormitory."

Turley became the roommate of Davis Love, Jr., and was one of my boys for the next four years.

Thirty years later Ed, a successful attorney, was taking his son, Greg, on a tour of colleges. Greg was graduating from Austin High, but he had his eye on going to one of the fine schools in Virginia or North Carolina.

Ed picked up his son at the airport in Washington, D.C., and they drove to Burning Tree and asked Max Elbin, the pro, if they could play a round. Max was polite to them, but he didn't get them onto the course. He said they might try again Sunday morning, if they were determined.

Early Sunday morning, Ed and Greg were in the Burning Tree pro shop, waiting for Max to come out of his office.

Greg was handling the clubs on the racks, picking them up, waggling them. Max opened the door of his office and said, "Listen, I'm sorry, but we're really crowded today, and I don't see how . . ."

Max stopped talking. He had noticed the way young Greg was handling the clubs.

"Anyone with a grip like yours can play on my course. Get your clubs and go to the tee," Max told them.

Ed and Greg thanked him and started out, but Max stopped them.

"You know, during World War II I was stationed at Bergstrom Air Force Base in Austin," Max said. "I went by the old Austin Country Club and asked Harvey Penick if he could get me onto his golf course. Harvey told me no.

"But before I left," Max continued, "I picked up a few clubs in the pro shop and handled them, gripped

24

them, fiddled with them. In a minute, Harvey Penick walked over to me. I was afraid he was going to remind me I was supposed to be leaving."

But what I had said to Max was, "Son, anyone with a grip like yours can play on my course. Get your clubs and go to the tee."

Ed told me that when Max heard Ed had played for me in college, Max not only got them onto Burning Tree, he also picked up their tab and invited them to lunch.

That's what a good grip can do for you.

Keeping the Edge

IN THE YEARS when Tom Kite and Ben Crenshaw were going around our Austin Country Club course near Riverside Drive nearly every day, I would say we had as many low-handicap players as any club in the country.

I was walking toward the practice tee one morning when I overheard a guest telling one of our members, "I don't get it. Why do I see all these good players out here taking lessons and practicing? What a waste of time and money. If I was a good player, I'd skip the lessons and practice and just go straight to the tee."

I wondered what this fellow might say to a great violinist. "Why bother with teachers and practice? You're such a good player, why don't you just play concerts only?"

I have known many golfers who could lay off the game for months at a time, maybe even for a year or more, and still go out and shoot in the 70s.

But I've never known one who could lay off for months and continue to play consistently at a championship level. Bobby Jones would rack his clubs in the storeroom for months in the winter and then he would go win an Open, but not without first taking time for intense practice sessions with his teacher, Stewart Maiden.

One of my scratch players left our club and moved to Kansas City. A couple of years later he came to me for a lesson.

Before we started, I asked what his problem was.

"My game is going downhill," he said. "I'm playing to a 3 handicap now. I want to get back to scratch and stay there."

I watched him hit iron shots for about ten minutes. I handed him his driver, and he pounded the ball long and down the middle.

"Well?" he said. "What am I doing wrong?"

"How often do you play golf?" I asked.

"Once a week is all I have time for anymore."

I said, "There's the answer. You need to play more. It's unreasonable for you to play once a week and expect to stay at scratch. From what I've seen today, you hit the ball as well as ever. But no once-a-week player can expect to maintain the scoring touch you need for scratch golf."

"There's nothing you can do for me?" he said.

I said yes, there was something I could do for him. I would go to the shop and line up a game for him with some other good players.

"This is the medicine you need," I said. "And you'll enjoy it while you're taking it."

Point of View

A QUESTION I liked to ask my college players was this: If you have just made putts of eight feet on six consecutive greens, and then you are faced with an eight-footer on the next hole to win the match, will you sink it?

Many of them said they might sink it, but they would be thinking the law of averages was against them, so there was a good chance they also might miss it.

My favorite answer was the one from George McCall during his sophomore year.

"I will make it, for sure. If I've just sunk six in a row, I'm hot and there is no way in the world I can miss," he said.

Jackie's Way

THE FAIRWAYS AT Memorial Park were baked hard and bare by the sun for the Texas Open in 1952.

Most of the players were having difficulty with their approach shots off ground that was about as unforgiving as your kitchen floor. We had a long and terrible drought during the early 1950s, and everything suffered from it, not least our golf courses.

But young Jack Burke, Jr., son of one of golf's finest and most influential teachers, laid his approach shots stiff for enough birdies to win the tournament.

Jackie's way was if he was within fifty yards of the green with an open shot, he used his putter.

He rolled his balls up to the flag consistently.

The Texas Wedge was not a secret weapon, of course. The other players in the tournament tried to use it, too. But Jackie was the best by far.

I remember Jimmy Demaret saying, "Hey, the kid is magic. I don't know how to explain it."

Talking about that tournament years later, Jackie revealed that the magic had been his imagination.

He said, "I would imagine that the whole fifty yards from my ball to the flag was all a giant green. Then I'd just hit a long lag putt to the hole.

"The other guys were thinking of the shot as using a putter out of the fairway and approaching onto the green. That picture made it into a harder shot. It was both an approach and a putt.

"In my mind, it was just one shot—a long putt."

Jackie, I should add, was a wonderful putter.

After Horton Smith and before Crenshaw, Burke was considered the best putter of his time.

I remember the note Jackie left in the locker of his cousin, David Marr, at Laurel Valley on the morning of the last round of the PGA National in 1965. Marr was tied with Tommy Aaron for the lead. Jack Nicklaus and Billy Casper were two strokes away.

The note said, "Fairways and greens, cous."

David shot a solid 71 and brought the championship home to Houston, where the Marrs and the Burkes are kinfolk.

Leaping Lucifer

THERE WAS A loud thunderstorm during the night.

Lightning cracked a limb off one of the giant oak trees that helped to make our golf course near Riverside Drive such a joy. We had many oaks I couldn't wrap my arms halfway around. They called our country road Riverside Drive because it followed the course of the Colorado River through the southeast part of town, but the road had been a cattle trail, and our golf course had been a dairy farm. A golf course needs water and good soil. The rolling farmland was excellent soil, and the thunderstorm was bringing us water. That night four or five inches of rain pounded the roof of our house a few yards from the twelfth tee.

Lord knows, we needed the rain. I never in my life complained about rain. Texas always needs rain, even when it is flooding. All natural-born Texans who have been on earth a while have endured long spells of no rain and have learned that a lot of rain always beats a drought.

At first light, I watched from our kitchen window, looking down the fairway to the green of the par-3 twelfth as the rain stopped. I knew the lone creek that meandered through the course would be churning along out of its banks, and the caddies would be swimming in the ponds that formed in the swales. It would be at least noon before we could open for play.

There was plenty of work to do at the club, but I

decided the rain had given me freedom to slip off and hit a bag of balls. I had a couple of lessons to give in the afternoon, and I wanted to practice my trick shots that I showed off at clinics and in exhibitions at baseball parks. Some of my pupils, especially the girls, would ask me to hit trick shots for them, and I needed to keep my touch.

I put away my polished shoes and my trousers with the fresh-pressed creases that I ordinarily wore to the club, and dressed in old clothes that wouldn't be ruined by the mud. By nine o'clock, my shop duties were under control, so I sneaked out to the tenth fairway with a bag of balls. I wanted to practice, not draw a crowd and wind up doing a show.

I dumped a mound of balls in the wet grass, paced off 145 yards down the fairway, and dropped the shag bag to be used as my target.

I had been hitting 7-irons for about five minutes when I noticed someone was leaning against a pecan tree, watching me from under the dripping branches.

A muddy Cadillac was parked on Grove Road, which runs beside the tenth fairway. I was already losing my hearing, and I wasn't aware the Cadillac had arrived.

"They told me up at the club that Harvey Penick might be down here," the fellow called from under the pecan tree branches.

"That's me." I was really wanting to practice, but this fellow was nobody from around Austin, and he caught my eye because he looked a little bit like the movie actor W. C. Fields.

Walking toward me, the fellow said, "I heard Harvey Penick is a classy dresser," as if my old clothes made him doubt he was talking to the right person.

I addressed the ball with my clubface upside down and backward. It appeared impossible to hit a shot from

30

that position. But I whacked a neat little draw that bounced up next to the shag bag.

"Good trick. I saw the Fat Man do it in Florida. You spin the grip in your hands faster than my eyes can follow it. Very nice," he said.

I looked the fellow over again. Bill Mehlhorn had told me about a big money player in Florida named the Fat Man.

"What's your name?" I asked.

"At my home club the boys call me Leaping Lucifer."

I smiled at that, but he didn't.

The fellow's nose wasn't as large as the movie actor's, but his face was flushed and plump with the expression of an angry baby. He was wearing a white silk shirt under a yellow cashmere sweater, and his trousers were creamy wool. He had on brown alligator shoes exactly like the pair I had left in the closet at home that morning. He was about the same age I was at the time, about fifty.

"I was hoping to get a lesson from you," he said. "I've driven all the way from New Orleans."

I said I could fit him in later in the day. He shook his head.

"I was hoping you could do it right now," he said. "I'm driving back this afternoon. I have a game at the club tomorrow morning. Please, pro, can I get my sticks out of the trunk? Tomorrow is my birthday, and I want to win."

"I don't promise I can help you," I said.

Before the words were out of my mouth, Leaping Lucifer was slogging across the fairway through the mud toward his Cadillac. I watched him open the trunk and wrestle with a leather bag that was big enough to carry three boys and a dog.

"Just bring your 7-iron," I yelled.

But he was already staggering back across the fairway, bent under the weight of the bag full of clubs, his alligator shoes squishing in the wet earth with each step. Mud was splashed all over his slacks and sweater. When he planted the bag beside me, it must have lowered three inches into the ground.

"Tomorrow's your birthday, is it?" I asked, to start him talking. Whatever demon had caused him to drive from New Orleans to Austin to seek help from a stranger, it might reveal itself if he talked about his life.

"Yeah. My fiancée is throwing a big party at the club tomorrow night. She organized a birthday tournament for me tomorrow afternoon."

"She sounds like a wonderful person," I said.

"I'm playing two guys a thousand bucks three ways, and five hundred with the other," he said.

I said, "I think you've come to the wrong teacher."

"I checked you out. You're the one. Dutch Harrison told me."

I said, "I'm happy to try to help you with your swing, but I've been known to fail, and I want no responsibility for what you win or lose at the tournament tomorrow. You'd better try a different pro."

"I didn't come to you because of the gambling money!" he cried, earnestly enough to make me believe him. "I came because I'm tired of being laughed at! Especially tomorrow! I don't want to be laughed at in front of my fiancée on my birthday!"

"What is it about you that is supposed to be so funny?" I asked.

"It's my golf swing!"

There was such misery and pleading in his voice that I told him to take out his 7-iron and address a mud clod as if it were a golf ball. His left-hand grip was very weak, rolled almost under the handle. With his right hand, he

32

held the club like a sledgehammer. Otherwise, his address was all right. He stood to the clod in a plain way, as I like to see.

"Make a few practice swings," I said.

He swung the club back and around at shoulder height, like a baseball bat. I was about to inform him that a true practice swing is always aimed at some spot on the ground so that it will imitate golf, but curiosity made me move on quickly to placing a golf ball on top of the mud clod.

"Hit it," I said.

The violent motion that followed startled me into dropping my club.

Maybe I can compare it to a man with an axe attacking a charging wild beast.

The fellow slashed his right shoulder and arm viciously toward the clod, and at the same time he lunged forward far past the ball—and yet, there was an explosion of mud, and I saw his 7-iron shot flying about six feet off the ground and slicing a little to bounce some ten yards short of my shag bag.

As a teacher with many years of experience, I have seen all sorts of leapers and lungers, but Leaping Lucifer was in a class by himself.

The most amazing thing about his swing was the exquisite timing that was necessary for him to produce a straight, usable, halfway decent 7-iron. Despite his plump cheeks and his middle-aged body, Leaping Lucifer was very talented as an athlete, or else he had just now been very lucky.

"Do it again," I said.

I stepped back a few feet to escape the shower of mud from his clubhead and his feet as he leaped and bashed the ball, his head finishing nearly waist high and two feet in front of his left leg.

But the ball landed within thirty feet of the first one.

"Can you hit your 7-iron like this consistently?" I asked.

"Yeah, pro. Pretty much. I don't hit the ball far, but I'm straight. Long carries over water or some kind of swamp or gully, those things kill me. I avoid those courses. I like a course where I can hit run up shots."

Remembering Lucifer all these years later, it occurs to me that he couldn't finish the first two holes at our Pete Dye golf course on the bank of the river we call Lake Austin. Lucifer's worm burners would never cross our ravines and water hazards. Most golf courses built in the 1980s went away from the old-fashioned ground game and forced players to hit the ball high. It would require a lifetime overhaul for Lucifer to hit a shot of much height. He could probably make it around the Old Course at St. Andrews with a score reasonably close to his handicap, and he could have finished a round at our Hancock Park or Riverside Drive courses, but his card at our new Austin Country Club would be a couple of X's followed by a brisk stroll back to the clubhouse.

"Are you going to help me?" he asked.

"What would you like me to do?"

"You can teach me to keep my head behind the ball so I look a little more stylish."

What he was asking for would take months, if it could be done at all.

"How often do you play golf?" I asked.

"Every Wednesday afternoon and usually on Sunday."

He was probably a doctor or a dentist. As a teacher, I had his best interest at heart, as I would expect from a doctor or dentist who was treating me. But this was like waiting until your disease was incurable or your teeth were falling out of your head before you went to see a professional.

"Do you practice your golf?" I asked.

"I hit a few balls before I go to the tee, just to warm up."

"What is your handicap?" I asked.

"I'm a 16."

I must have looked surprised that it was so low, because he misunderstood and scowled at me.

"I used to be a 12," he said. "But I was much younger then."

"How long have you swung at the ball this way?" I asked.

"Probably twenty-five years. I didn't take up the game until I could afford to join a country club."

He realized his alligator shoes were buried in the mud, and he pulled his feet free and moved to a patch of ground that was a little more solid. I knew he was waiting for me to do something wonderful for him, but I had already mentally discarded the things I would ordinarily do for a player who lunges. I would have started with his grip, but fixing this fellow's grip would have only made matters worse.

Leaping Lucifer glanced at his wristwatch.

"Just a couple more questions," I said. "These men you will be playing with tomorrow, can you beat them?"

"Yeah. All of them outhit me a long way off the tee, but with my handicap I win a lot more than I lose."

"Are you a good putter?" I asked.

"One of the best. If I need to sink a six-foot putt on the eighteenth green to win, I'll make it."

As the golf coach at the University of Texas, I told my boys to beware of the opponent who had both a bad grip and a bad swing, because chances are he repeated his mistakes consistently and had learned how to score. This was my diagnosis of Leaping Lucifer. Anything I did in one lesson to change his grip or his swing would destroy what he already believed and would cause him to lose all his bets tomorrow, a sorry birthday present.

"Listen, pro, I'd like to get started here," he said. "It's a tough twelve hours back to New Orleans."

I needed to give this fellow some kind of gift, something that would make him feel better about himself without ruining the only good thing about his swing, which was that he did it the same way over and over with impeccable timing.

Reflecting on the situation, I remembered Leaping Lucifer had not asked me to improve his golf game. He had asked me to make his swing look stylish, that's all. It was vanity. He had been swinging this way for twenty-five years, and he had been laughed at for probably as long. But he was a winner, so he had borne the burden of his opponents' wisecracks because he was taking their money.

Now his fiancée had entered the picture, and tomorrow was his birthday. He didn't want to be laughed at in front of her.

"You're a very lucky man," I said.

"Yeah?" He eyed me suspiciously. "How?"

"Well, you've got a new Cadillac car and a cashmere sweater and a woman who wants to marry you, plus you've made it through life in apparent good health for another year."

"Skip the sermon, pro. Let's talk about my golf swing. What are you going to do about it?"

"Nothing," I said.

"You give up, huh? It's that bad, is it?"

I took off my cap and scratched my head.

"In fact, I wouldn't touch your swing because you are a golfing genius. Your swing is not funny, it is unique to your particular genius. You play golf only once or twice a week, and you don't spend hours on the practice range.

To keep your game going at a 16-handicap level, and win money from your opponents with it, you must be a genius."

He was liking what he was hearing. It was making sense. Sure, I told him, if he had time to put in long practice sessions and play several days a week, as most of the best players did, he could get his game down into the high 70s. Good a putter as he was, his scores would only get better.

Leaping Lucifer was smiling at me now.

"If they laugh at you tomorrow, you just wink at your fiancée. She's a smart woman. She'll see that they're really laughing at themselves because they aren't good enough to beat you. You and your fiancée can have a fine laugh while you're counting your winnings."

"Ah, pro," he said, "I see what you mean. What do I care if these losers laugh? I'm the one who wins the game."

"One more thing," I said. "It's a tip for tomorrow and now on. When you hit pitch shots to the green, use your sand wedge, and grip it high on the handle, which prevents chili-dipping, and hold tight with the pinky and ring fingers of your left hand so the blade won't turn over. This will take three strokes off your game tomorrow."

This advice couldn't possibly hurt, and it would help if he remembered to do it. This was something technical enough for him to put his mind on it and feel he had learned something.

"Hey, great, thanks," he said brightly.

He wiped the mud off his right hand and stuck it out. I shook it.

"How much do I owe you?" he asked.

"Send 20 percent of your winnings to the Salvation Army," I said. "I hope your wedding is blessed forever. And say hello to Dutch Harrison for me."

I turned back to the pile of balls at my feet. Behind me I could hear the clanking and puffing as he heaved the heavy bag over his shoulder, and then the slurping of those beautiful alligator shoes sloshing through the mud on the fairway as Leaping Lucifer marched again to his Cadillac.

The Cadillac backed up and made a U-turn on Grove Road and I watched the sprays of water thrown up by its wheels as he drove happily off toward New Orleans.

I faded a 7-iron that landed with a loud plunk against the shag bag. I laughed and wiped my hands with a towel. It was a great morning to be alive and be teaching, and there were another fifty balls to hit before I would need to go back to the shop. That warm, easy feeling is hard to explain, but it is better than riches to me.

The Natural

I HAD BEEN teaching the game for several years, but I was new to being a university golf coach in 1931 when a black-haired boy named Ed White, from Bonham, Texas, started playing at the first Austin Country Club on a junior membership that his father had bought for fifteen dollars.

Ed was staying with his grandmother, who lived near our original club, one of the oldest golf courses in the country.

I learned later that Ed had taught himself to play golf

while caddying at the Bonham Country Club. Because he was a caddie, Ed wasn't allowed to play at the club, but he and four friends fashioned a six-hole layout of their own in a pasture. Ed read *The American Golfer* magazine and studied the photographs and drawings of Jones and Hagen and other great players. One day his father saw Ed playing golf in the pasture and recognized a natural talent. Soon Ed was on his way to Austin. He still had never met a golf pro, much less taken a lesson.

After Ed would come in from playing a round at Austin Country Club, members would ask what he shot. Nearly every time, Ed would reply with a number that was 65 or less.

We could see from his graceful, freewheeling swing that Ed was a good player. But 65 or better every time out? Several members suggested Ed must be at least hitting a mulligan or two. Our Hancock Park course was not a Pine Valley, but it was a legitimate golf course with some tight fairways and tricky greens. Nobody, we thought, could shoot 65 or less day after day.

Ed enrolled at the University of Texas as a petroleum engineering student. In February 1932, Ed turned out for our 72-hole qualifying tournament for the Texas golf team. The low six scores would make the squad, and from then on they would have challenge matches among themselves to determine their rankings from week to week.

In the tournament, Ed shot 61-64-65-62 and finished first by about a mile and a half.

His 72-hole total of 252 has never been threatened in the Massengill Trophy, which is given to the low qualifier on the Texas team.

By this time, I had started paying closer attention to him. He had as much talent for the game as anyone I ever saw. Until Jack Nicklaus came along, Ed White was the best long iron player in my lifetime. He hit his 1-iron about 230 yards as accurately as other players could hit a 75-yard wedge.

As a member of the Texas team, Ed received two golf balls a week as his stipend from the university.

I did nothing to try to change Ed's swing. He had a slight pause at the top. I would not teach anyone to pause at the top, but neither would I tell a player like Ed to stop pausing. That would have been like trying to change Babe Ruth's batting style.

Ed won the Southwest Conference individual title three years in a row in 1933, '34 and '35. One other player in history has won three in a row—Ben Crenshaw. Another University of Texas boy, National Amateur champion Justin Leonard, won the conference individual trophy four times in succession after rules were changed to make freshmen eligible.

In the National Intercollegiate, Ed lost in the finals his junior year, but as a senior he became the first Texas player to be national champion when he beat Fred Haas in the finals at Congressional in Washington, D.C. Many years later Fred Haas, who had become a top touring pro, walked into my golf shop and saw Ed White's photograph on the wall. "I'll never forget that man," Fred told me. "He's the best player I ever saw."

It was thirty-six years before a Texas player won the national title again. Ben Crenshaw won it in 1971 and 1972 and tied for the championship in 1973 with his teammate, Tom Kite.

Ed finished his senior year by winning the Mexican Amateur, defeating Johnny Dawson 10 and 8 in the thirty-six-hole finals.

Ed was very long off the tee. He hit the ball at least fifteen yards past the best amateurs he faced. In my opinion, the young Ed White was as long as Ben Hogan or Byron Nelson in their prime.

In 1936 Ed played on the Walker Cup team and won all his matches at Pine Valley. He was paired in the foursomes with Reynolds Smith.

People ask Ed, who is retired in Kingsland, Texas, and plays golf three times a week, why he didn't turn professional and take advantage of his talent.

The answer is that Ed had a wife and was offered a good job with Gulf Oil, and the pro tournament money in those days was way too low to lure him into the life of a golfing gypsy on the tour. During Ed's senior year, Gene Sarazen won the Masters and was paid seven hundred dollars as his prize. The country was into the Great Depression, and the Whites were having babies.

If Ed had gone out and played against the professionals, I believe he would have been the best of his time.

Gulf sent Ed to Houston, where he joined Houston Country Club. He won the Houston Invitational at Memorial Park twice. In 1950, Ed faced Morris Williams, Jr., the best Texas player since Ed had been the king sixteen years earlier, in the second round of the Houston tournament. Ed beat Morris, 5 and 4.

Ed was so good and so confident that he would aim through a hole in the trees instead of taking a safe way around, and it was rare for him to miss.

I asked him how he developed his golf swing, and he said, "I come back as far as I can and then I hit it as hard as I can." He had tremendously fast hands and a powerful weight shift that was a joy to watch.

A few years ago I was sitting in my golf cart at the new Austin Country Club, our Pete Dye course, when a tall fellow walked up and said, "Remember me?"

I said, "You still have that little pause at the top of your swing?"

Ed White looked surprised. I hadn't seen him in more than forty years.

"You still remember that?" he said.

A natural like Ed White, I could never forget.

The Barbed Wire Line

IF YOU ARE having trouble coming over the top a little bit, or you find a tendency to flinch from the blow and hit up on an iron shot, or your downswing is from too steep an angle, there is a mental picture that may cure your problems.

Imagine that there is a line of barbed wire that starts from far behind your ball and goes all the way to your target.

The barbed wire is a few inches off the ground in your imaginary picture. The wire passes over your ball and aims directly at where you want your ball to go.

You must hit the ball without lashing and scratching your club against the barbed wire. The only way you can do this is by swinging from inside to square to inside and by staying down with the shot at impact.

Give this a try on the practice range, not during a golf game. If you practice it, you won't need to think about it while you are playing—unless something goes wrong with your swing in the middle of a round. Then you might walk off by yourself a little way and make a few practice swings at a tee, imagining the barbed wire line.

One of the better amateurs the University of Texas produced, Kirby Attwell, told me that he still uses the barbed wire line in his mind during practice sessions at River Oaks in Houston, where Kirby has been club champion about ten times.

Imagining barbed wire makes some pupils nervous. To them, I say to imagine a line drawn on the ground that runs over the ball from behind and goes all the way to the target. Swinging back and swinging down, you should feel you are inside the line.

Make the Course a Pleasure

―――――――――

I HAVEN'T BEEN able to travel for several years, but from looking at television and talking to friends and pupils, I agree with Jackie Burke, Jr., when he said, "God is going to make a lot of these golf course architects answer for what they have done to the land."

It's not just some of the architects who are to blame for a decade or more of building golf courses that are tricked up by artificial difficulties such as bulldozer-dug water hazards where water is not meant to be and bunkers that catch only the less skilled players. Real estate developers and greens committees have spoiled more golf courses than architects, who, like other artists, do best if left alone.

A pupil told me that while on vacation in Arizona, he and his wife lost fourteen golf balls in the water during two rounds at a famous resort course. I said, "You must have been pretty wild. The last time I was in Arizona, I didn't see any water."

No, the pupil said, this course even had a roaring waterfall.

"We had a good time at the course because it was our vacation and an adventure, but it is way too hard for us," the pupil said. "My wife and I agreed if we had to play that course every day, we would quit golf."

If lakes or rivers or creeks or wetlands, or for that matter the ocean, are natural to the area, they should be used in golf design so that nature is enhanced rather than destroyed. Ponds are needed for drainage, and these can make the course more pleasing to the eye, or they can be hidden away.

But I see water in front of many greens on modern courses just so the holes will look pretty on a postcard. It's not much fun for a high handicapper to play regularly on a course that has no proper entry to the greens. By proper entry, I mean a route where the ball can be bounced onto the putting surface.

Anybody with enough money to spend can design a course that is terribly difficult. The genius in golf architecture is to be able to build a course that is enjoyable for high handicappers but is cleverly bunkered and ponded so as to cause problems for the experts. An example that comes to mind at once is Augusta National, but there are many others that are accessible to the public, like any course by Donald Ross or Alister MacKenzie.

Architect A. W. Tillinghast, who built prominent courses that have stood the test of time, told about his conversation with a member of a club where a real estate developer had hired an architect to build a course that would draw national attention.

"Nobody has ever broken par at our course," the member bragged.

Tillinghast replied, "Why? What's wrong with the place?"

Crushed by Crunch

A PUPIL NAMED Townsend from California told me this story one summer while I was teaching at Cherry Hills.

Townsend was playing in an amateur match-play tournament at North Berwick in Scotland. He hired a local caddie who was known as Crunch.

Townsend and Crunch set out on a practice round the day before the tournament. It was Townsend's first visit to North Berwick, and he was awed by treading the ground that had been walked on by many of the giants of the game since the invention of golf. I have heard Ben Crenshaw say he thinks North Berwick is one of the best courses in the world.

Townsend said his feeling of reverence crept into his game and elevated him to heights he didn't know he was capable of. With Crunch trudging along beside him, selecting clubs for him and pointing out the proper places to aim and reading the greens, Townsend played the finest round of his life. The wind blew hard off the sea, as it is supposed to at North Berwick, and rain showers struck a couple of times, but Townsend marched bravely through the elements and holed a birdie putt at the eighteenth to finish two over par.

Townsend gave Crunch a handsome tip and arranged to meet him at the North Berwick golf shop the next morning for the beginning of the tournament.

"Do you know this fellow called Liam Flaherty?" Townsend asked the caddie.

"Aye," said Crunch.

"Tell me about him," Townsend said.

"Ah, he's no good," replied Crunch in his East Lothian dialect. "He's no good with his driver. He's no good with his irons. He's no good with his putter. He's just flat no good at all."

Townsend beamed at this news. "Flaherty is my opponent in the first round tomorrow."

"Ah," said Crunch. "He'll beat you."

Mental Cases

ALL SEASONED PLAYERS know that golf is a state of mind.

How you think and how you use your emotions while traveling the golf course is the difference between playing to the best of your ability and hacking it around with a frown on your face.

Where Your Hands
Should Be

———

I HAVE A letter from a friend in Ponte Vedra Beach, Florida. It is written on stationery from the Sawgrass Country Club. My friend says his club "is the hard course, not the one nearby that the pros play on television."

The older Sawgrass is twenty-seven holes divided into West, East and South nines that have the Atlantic Ocean winds to change their character. The Scots long ago welcomed the sea winds into their course layouts, and the top architects always have taken the wind direction and velocity into account in their creations.

But what my friend's letter is about is the address, and I think a little bit is about the mind game.

He says: "A guy I regularly play with told me recently that at address my hands are too far from my body. I had never thought about my hands in relation to my body. My playing companion says my hands at address should be a fist and a half out in front of my crotch.

"Sure enough, my golf game went to pieces. I can't stop thinking about my hands. At first I thought my so-called friend had put this crazy idea in my mind so I would stop winning all the skins and Nassaus from him, which is exactly what happened.

"But I started watching the pros on TV. Most of them

do seem to carry their hands about a fist and a half in front of their crotches, or toward the inside of their left thighs. However, there are some whose hands almost touch their thighs, and others who reach out another six inches. I saw a videotape of Moe Norman, the amazing Canadian, who sticks his arms and hands way out at address and hits the ball straighter than anybody in the world.

"Now I am even more confused than usual. Where should I put my hands at address, distance-from-bodywise?"

Let me tell you an easy remedy that will last the rest of your life.

Stand up. Hold your arms straight out in front, chest high, with your right arm stretching a little farther than your left, so that when you clap your palms together the fingertips of the left hand don't quite reach the fingertips of the right hand. Be sure there is no tension in your arms.

Now, spread your feet about shoulder-width apart in a golf stance. Flex your knee slightly. Bend forward from your hips. Be balanced. Feel athletic.

Keeping your palms together, let your arms fall naturally in front of your body.

Your hands are now in the correct place for your build. Look at your hands. Make a note of where they are. I mean, write it down, so that later when your memory wanders you can come back and read where your hands should be.

When you measure the distance from your body to your hands, you may find it really is a fist and a half. Or maybe more. Or maybe less. Whatever the distance, now you know the right place for your hands for a regular shot for once and for all.

The next trick is to stop thinking about the position of your hands.

I remember an old story about a schoolmaster who told a pupil to go stand in the corner and stay until he could quit thinking about a white bear. The child stayed there all day. When the teacher planted the picture of a white bear in the youngster's mind, the white bear was there to live.

Through my years at Austin Country Club, most of the powerful and rich men in Texas have played here at some time or other. I know many a golfer who is the boss of a big, successful company but who has the mind of a child when it comes to golf. Let a companion suggest that this tough executive is flying his right elbow on the backswing, and it won't be long before I am asked to give a lesson about a flying right elbow that might not ever have flown if someone hadn't suggested it.

The only way to get the white bear or the flying elbow or the position of your hands out of your thoughts is to concentrate your thoughts on something else.

Now that you have discovered where your hands are supposed to be, concentrate on where you want the ball to go. That is a positive thought to occupy your mind and bring positive results.

Rock Solid Putting

———

EVERY TIME I see a touring pro miss a short putt on television, I see a head moving.

The average player misses short putts because of poor

speed, poor aim, and an off-center hit, as well as a moving head.

But the expert is a good judge of speed and line and is able to stroke the putter so as to hit the ball solidly, or he or she wouldn't be an expert.

Moving your head or your eyes on a short putt is a result of fear or of carelessness, and it is a fault that has lost many a tournament.

To the Finish

STEWART MAIDEN'S FAMOUS advice to Bobby Jones that "you don't hit the ball with your backswing" has been on my lips with many pupils.

For sixty years I have seen a parade of high-handicap pupils who somehow learned the swing the wrong way around. Rather than learning that what counts is the way the club goes through the ball, these pupils seem to believe they will receive style points for a lovely backswing regardless of what happens next.

Once the backswing is set in a correct position, these pupils act as if the job is done rather than just begun, and all sorts of unnecessary movements follow. The club will probably go out and over, cut across the ball in a glancing blow with little power, and wind up somewhere about breast high, usually as the pupil struggles to keep balance.

Fascinated by a well-done backswing, the pupil congratulates himself and then turns the critical function of striking the ball over to random actions.

A proper finish is the bookend to a good backswing. If you swing to a nicely balanced follow-through, what happens to the ball in the hitting area will be a success.

There is no aspirin to give for this problem that will make everybody feel better in an hour.

I believe the best approach for a teacher faced with this situation is to start the pupil's swing at a good, high, balanced finish, and proceed backward.

This will take time. One lesson is not enough to begin curing this fault, so I would try to teach something different but helpful, like clipping the tee, unless the pupil would promise to practice hard and come see me again.

If the pupil is willing to put in the study and practice, I ask the pupil to pose in a perfect follow-through, elbows out in front of the body, facing the target with the left foot carrying all the weight, head up and eyes looking down range to follow a good shot.

Once the pupil gets the feeling of what a good finish position feels like, I say, "Now I want you to make a swing that concludes in this exact position. Pay no attention to your backswing for now. We don't care if it is too long or across the line or too short or just right. Just take the club back slowly and make a swing that finishes in this balanced follow-through position."

I repeat, "The good finish shows what has gone on before it."

At a teaching seminar years ago, a British pro demonstrated how he taught the swing by starting at the ball and pushing it forward with the clubhead until it rolled away and then the pupil went on into a full finish.

The pro said the backswing was a natural thing that would come easily once the pupil learned the route and destination of the foreswing.

51

Let me add that a teacher must watch that his pupil swings into a good finish that is real and not faked. I don't mind if the pupil falls back a little bit now and then, but I don't like to see one ever fall forward.

You may be thinking that when you watch golf on television, especially the Senior Tour, you see a lot of abrupt follow-throughs. But remember that these are experts with years of experience, and they know how to move the club through the hitting area, and also their backswings tend more toward three-quarters than full. In many golf shots the backswing and the forward swing are the same length.

But the Senior Tour is still the home of classic swings that have stood the test of time, as well as classic sluggers who have been winners for decades.

Older players are always telling me they can't take the club back as far as they once did. But that's not really their problem. Their problem is they can't swing the club as far forward as they once did.

Take a golf club or a walking cane or a broomstick and pose in front of the mirror in your bedroom. Put yourself into the finish position that you see the experts finish in. Hold yourself there, weight on your left foot, belt buckle pointing to the target. You look as good as Ben Hogan, don't you? Enjoy it as if you are watching a long, powerful shot sail down the fairway. Memorize it, and take that feeling to the golf course with you.

Have Fun

————

WHEN I SAY to have fun on the golf course, what I mean is to take pleasure in the game and in your companions and your surroundings. Whether you are at Pebble Beach or pulling your trolley at Rancho Park, be mindful that you are in a special place. Be aware of the trees and the sky and the feel of the earth under your feet. Listen to the byplay of your companions. Breathe deeply. Forget the stock market. Enjoy yourself fully while you are inside the boundaries of the golf course, a world of its own.

To me fun does not mean dancing and singing down the fairways, creating a hullabaloo and telling loud jokes. This behavior might be amusing at a summer camp, but I believe it does not fit with the game of golf.

I believe playing golf can bring you happiness.

Golf will put you into pleasant associations with other people. You can play golf with your children. You can play golf with your wife or husband. You can play with your pals at the regular course. Or you can just show up at some strange municipal course, and the starter will fit you into a game, and within an hour you will feel you have known these people all your life.

You can learn more about your companions in one round of golf than in years of parties and dinners. You can learn in one round whether you really want to play golf—or do business—with that person again.

I suggest you always have a little competition going to

keep your attention sharp. You don't have to bet money, though I certainly do approve of a good money game. If you are playing with your children, let's say the winner will watch the others wash the car. With your wife or husband, the stakes could be dinner at a good restaurant. If it's a muddy day, the loser can clean the winner's shoes.

It's perfectly okay to play just for the love of the game. Going around the course by yourself early in the morning or late in the evening, hitting a mulligan if you feel like it, is a satisfying use of time.

Because of the handicap system and the different sets of tees, you can make a golf match with anybody.

Golf has it over tennis in this respect. A good tennis player can't have much fun matched against a novice, and the novice won't enjoy being embarrassed. This may make for good exercise, but it is no game.

As a starter at the club, I would try politely to persuade the players to use the tees that would fit their games and allow them to perform to the best of their ability.

Vanity comes into play here. To me it seems golf makes no sense if you're a weak hitter but insist on using the back sets of tees, as so many men do. Where is the fun in watching your drive fall into a barranca, or hitting 3-woods to the par-4 greens?

In the early days of our Pete Dye course, which is very difficult even if you are on the correct set of tees, I used to see players heading toward the Gold tees on the first hole, and I would call to them, "Those tees are for Tom Kite and Ben Crenshaw."

Put your mind at ease at the golf course and have fun. Golf is a game for everyone, not just for the talented few.

No matter how poorly you play, there is always someone you can beat. No matter how well you play, there is always someone who can beat you.

Matters of Style

EVERYBODY WHO KNOWS me knows I admire a beautiful golf grip. I would never tire of looking at the hands of Mickey Wright or Ben Crenshaw or Horton Smith or Tommy Armour on the handle of a club. The sight of a beautiful grip moves me like a masterpiece of art.

But I know my definition of a beautiful grip does not fit all fingers or all players' styles.

There is more to a good grip than beauty.

Sometimes the attitude with which the club is gripped tells me more about what a player is made of than the positioning of his hands.

The sense of confidence and ability, the manner in which the player sets up over the ball, and then the flight of the ball itself—these are also beautiful to me.

Beauty is important, and the fundamentals are important, but appearance is far outweighed by how different conditions are responded to and what is the result.

Not for one moment would I consider suggesting to Paul Azinger that he move his hands to a more fundamental position so they would fit my personal favorite idea of a beautiful grip.

As I always told my college boys who complained

when they lost a match to someone they considered eccentric, "Maybe it wasn't an accident. Pretty is as pretty does."

Under Pressure

———

WHEN YOU ARE under pressure in a tournament or a match, or even when you are under the pressure of hitting off the first tee at your Saturday morning game with a crowd watching, just go up and make the best swing you can make rather than trying to be someone else or doing something you really down deep know is beyond your ability.

There is one technical tip I can give you for dealing with pressure around the greens: use the correct club. Select the club that will land the ball on the green and get it rolling the soonest. That's your most pressure-proof shot.

Sending for John

———

THERE WAS A boy at Rice named John Garrett who could hit the ball like a pro but was studying to be a dentist, which is what he became.

One year we were holding the Southwest Conference individual tournament in Austin, and I noticed John was nowhere to be seen when his tee time approached.

I phoned Jess Neely, the Athletic Director at Rice. Jess told me he thought the tournament was tomorrow. John was in class at that moment.

"Well," I said, "if you'll put John on a plane and get him up here, I'll have one of my boys go around with him. John deserves to play in this tournament."

John won the tournament and went on to play for the Walker Cup team and set himself up in a successful dental practice.

I wonder if the rules today would allow what Jess and I did the day John didn't show up.

A Good Day at Cherry Hills

DURING ONE OF the summers I taught at Cherry Hills, I was having a difficult time with a pupil whose downswing was coming over the top. I was using all my wiles to teach her how to bring her clubface into the ball from the inside to square and then back inside, but there was something in her head that kept her swinging from outside to inside.

We paused for a chat. On a pleasant, sunny day in Denver, I would sometimes give as many as twenty lessons. I preferred it this way, because I could spend as much or as little time with a pupil as I thought would help. Some pupils needed five minutes. There were others I spent ten hours with—not all in one day, to be sure—and sometimes still failed to put them on the right path.

The woman pupil and I walked over to get a drink of water at Cherry Hills. I asked her, "Might it be that there is something on your mind that is bothering you?"

She looked away, a worried frown crossing her face, and said, "Why would you ask?"

"I don't mean to be prying into your personal life," I said. "I'm wondering if you are too distracted to listen to what I have been telling you. If your mind is elsewhere right now, let's call it off and try again another day."

She said, "No, I'm fine, really. I'm trying to do what you say. I'm trying to stay behind the ball and keep my shoulders level in my swing and . . ."

As she paused for a sip of water, I asked, "When did I tell you to keep your shoulders level when you swing?"

"Wasn't that you?" she said. "Well, anyway, everybody knows you're supposed to."

We walked back to our place on the range. I asked her to hit another 7-iron for me.

Her downswing came over the top again, but now it was clear to me where the problem was.

"What is it that you swing your shoulders level with?" I asked.

"Well, you know. Level."

"Do you mean level as in level with the horizon?" I asked.

"Sure. Level as in horizontal. I was taught that swinging my shoulders level is a fundamental," she said.

I asked her to address another ball. I went around behind her and placed my hands on her shoulders.

58

"Listen to me and think about what I'm saying," I said.

I asked her to make a slow-motion swing while I kept my hands on her shoulders.

When she started her right shoulder around in line with the horizon in her forward swing, I gripped her shoulders tightly and said, "Stop."

I guided her again to the top of her backswing.

"You misunderstood the teaching to swing your shoulders on a horizontal level," I said. "Horizontal means your shoulders turn horizontal with your posture. Horizontal with your spine. Not horizontal with the horizon. Let's try it again."

With my hands on her shoulders, she bent forward from the hips and kept her back straight and went through a slow-motion swing.

When she turned into her follow-through, she smiled as if I had suddenly given her an incredible gift.

"That's it!" she said. "I understand! Level with my spine, not with the edge of the world!"

I stepped around in front again. I watched her settle into address. She struck her 7-iron smartly, swinging from inside to down the line and back to the inside.

It gave me a shiver of pleasure, and I moved on along the range to where another pupil was warming up, waiting for me. I loved those long summer days at Cherry Hills.

Your Game Can Fit
the Course

FEW GOLFERS WHO shoot 80 or more can make the ball hook or slice on purpose with accuracy or consistency.

Yet you will see a 15-handicapper come to a par 4 that doglegs to the left around a big oak, pull out his driver and say, "I'll just hook it around that tree down there," even though his natural shot is closer to a slice.

This golfer is allowing the course designer to force him to play a game that makes the golfer uncomfortable.

If the golfer does manage to hit a hook off the tee, chances are it will be a wild one into the woods, and the woes have begun.

What I would say to the higher handicapper is, "Turn the tables on the designer. Make the course fit the game you know how to play."

Suppose you are faced with a dogleg left around a big oak tree. Leave your driver in the bag. Pull out your 3-wood and hit it down the right side of the fairway. Probably the big oak tree will remain in your way.

Plan your second shot to cut off the angle and open up the green. Your second shot may be a medium or short iron. For sure, your third shot will be a short pitch or chip to the hole. You have a good putt at a par, no worse than a bogey. You are, after all, an 85-shooter playing to your handicap.

What you have avoided is the high number or the X you would get by hooking your drive into the woods.

Suppose you, the 85-shooter, come to a par 5 that has a carry of 125 yards over rocks and brush and cactus in Arizona or high grass in Scotland or water in Florida or a canyon at our Pete Dye layout at Austin Country Club.

A carry of this distance is not noticed by the expert. But you are a high handicapper. It enters your mind that it is not out of the question you could top this drive or pop it up. Your companions are reaching for their drivers. What do you do?

If you have even a sniff of a doubt, hit the shot off the tee that you know will carry your ball over the trouble and drop it in the fairway. Maybe the right club is your favorite 6-iron that fills you with confidence.

You will avoid penalty strokes, lost balls and long delays. As a solid 85-shooter, you can reach the green in two or three more shots for your par or bogey.

Golf courses used to be strategic in design. They played harder than they looked. Then it became the fashion to design golf courses that look impossible and play too hard for the average golfer.

I shake my head in wonder at the high-handicap guests who come to our club and want to play from the Gold tees all the way back so they can "see it all." For them, "all" would be the bottoms of ravines with an occasional glimpse of the sky.

The same guest will leave complaining that our course is unfair. But the guest has brought his punishment upon himself. It is a matter of cause and effect.

We have five sets of tees. Our course is beautiful and inviting if you let yourself play from the tees that fit your ability.

This also will make the course fit your game.

Fairway Bunker Play

A GIRL WHO was trying to make the golf team at the University of Texas came to me for a checkup. I watched her hit a few shots, and her swing looked good. I asked which part of her game needed attention.

"Oh, it's those fairway bunkers," she said. "Every time I hit into a fairway bunker, it costs me a stroke or two."

"How much time do you spend practicing that shot?" I asked.

From the expression on her face, I believe she had never in her life thought of doing such a thing.

"Where would I practice a fairway bunker shot?" she said. "I'd have to go out on the course to find a fairway bunker to hit out of, but the course is always full of players."

She had me on that count. I don't know of a practice range that has a fairway bunker in which a player can practice the long shots out of the sand.

I'm sure I will later be informed of many practice ranges that have fairway bunkers for full shots, but I can't think of one right now, nor could I when I was trying to help the college girl, Jenny Turner.

"Let's sit and talk about it," I said.

I told her that she was a good swinger who could handle fairway bunkers if she adopted a realistic attitude.

"Make a plan for your shot," I said. "Select a target that you are sure is within your ability. On a par 4, your target may not be the green. You should aim for a safe landing with a shot left to the pin."

As to the hitting of the bunker shot, there are a few simple things to keep in mind.

Make certain you choose a club with enough loft to clear the lip of the bunker. Grip tightly with the ring and little fingers of your left hand to prevent the clubface from rolling shut.

You need a firm, balanced stance at address. If you have a good lie in the bunker, play the ball in the same position you would use in the fairway. Aim at your target and pick the ball clean with your swing.

The plan changes if your lie is partly buried in the sand. Then your objective is to get out of the bunker and onto the fairway, even if it requires a sand wedge.

Hitting out of a fairway bunker is not a shot to fear if you keep your expectations realistic. Unless your name is Hale Irwin, you are probably not going to knock the ball 220 yards onto the green from a bunker. But you can certainly advance your ball toward the hole.

You may have to practice this shot only in your mind, but fortunately that is where good golf comes from.

Greenside Bunkers

IT IS SURPRISING to me how many golfers play the game for years without ever getting over their fear of what is one of the easiest shots in the game—the explosion, or chip, or even putt, out of a greenside bunker.

After Gene Sarazen made the sand wedge popular

and greens committees started having the sand raked smooth on their courses, the greenside bunker shot became almost too easy for expert players.

I would like to see a professional tournament in which all bunkers—greenside or fairway—are left unraked, just to put the difficulty back into it.

A high handicapper who is terrified of a greenside sand shot will think, oh yeah, if the shot is so easy how come I can't do it?

You can do it if you will use the method I describe. It is the method used by Tom Kite, who is as good from a bunker as any player in history. Use Tom's method and go to a practice bunker and hit twenty-five balls. You will discover it is easy. Your fear will be gone forever.

Open the blade of your sand wedge before you take your grip. Place your hands high on the handle as you would for a full swing. Gripping down on the handle leads to quitting on the shot. Squeeze with the ring and little fingers of your top hand to prevent the blade from closing at contact with the sand.

Point the shaft at your crotch with your hands slightly ahead of the ball. Take a square stance with the ball in the middle of your stance and your clubface aimed to the right of the pin, if that is your target.

Now move your left foot, hips and shoulders to the left until your clubface is aiming directly at the target. Lean a little extra weight onto your left foot.

Make a normal swing along the line established by your shoulders. Hit the sand an inch or more behind the ball, depending on the distance to cover, and the ball will fly up in a shower of sand and plop onto the green.

It's a simple shot if you practice it.

But the explosion is not the only way out of a greenside bunker. In some instances, a chip may be called for where there is no lip to conquer. Or perhaps you will reach for your putter.

At the Los Angeles Open one year at Lakeside, I was down in a bunker in a deep hollow way below the green, and my inner voice told me to give the ball a whack with my putter. To knowledgeable watchers in the gallery, a putter may have looked to be a poor choice. But from where I stood, there was no shot that looked better than the putter, and I learned long ago to listen to that little voice.

My ball ran all the way up the side of the bunker and rolled onto the green within a few feet of the hole for a par.

I heard Harry Cooper say, "Those Texas men with their Texas Wedges—it's not fair."

The precision with which Tommy Kite hits his wedges out of sand bunkers beside the green is so consistent that it doesn't look fair to high handicappers who live in fear of the shot.

But if you learn to approach the shot the way Tom does, and hit one bag of balls out of a practice bunker, you will soon see how easy it is.

The Left Wrist

———

THE ONLY THING the left wrist must do in the golf swing is hang on to the handle without flapping or slapping. The snap in the golf swing is caused by the rolling of the forearms, not the wrists.

The hands must stay ahead of the clubface at impact on every shot. With a pitch, chip or putt, the hands remain ahead of the clubface into the follow-through.

More pros have asked me to check them in this area than any other during the years.

For high handicappers, collapsing the left wrist on a full swing means instant loss of power.

It is disaster when the right arm takes over the swing. The misuse of the right arm ruins many a swing. Often this is caused by a weak grip. The left arm must control the swing and keep the club on the proper path while the right adds power.

When I was golf coach at the university, many of my boys came from West Texas, where they learned to play in hard wind on dry ground. Hardly a one of them ever hit from the top or flapped his left wrist. They had very strong grips and hit the ball from way inside, producing a low burning tail hook that ran forever. You won with this shot in West Texas, but you couldn't break 90 with it at Colonial Country Club.

My old friend Billy Penn, a fine player for many years now, remembers those West Texas boys. "There were half a dozen players in West Texas who could have beaten Jack Nicklaus if they'd wanted to hit that chicken fade," Billy told me, grinning at his joke.

By trial and error, studying the West Texas grips and modifying them on my players, I noticed that as the grip got weaker there was a tendency for the left wrist to break down.

I wish I could find an immediate cure for the flapping left wrist, but I haven't. The most valuable thing I can say about it is that you should use a strong grip and rotate your left arm on the downswing, and your left wrist should do the correct thing on its own.

A Visit with Young Hal

I WAS DOING the inventory in the golf shop one morning when I got a phone call from a Louisiana oil man named Howard Sutton.

Howard told me he had a sixteen-year-old son, Hal. It had been Howard's ambition that Hal would grow up to play middle linebacker for Howard's old friend Frank Broyles, football coach at Arkansas.

But Hal had picked up a set of golf clubs and had gone out and played fifty-four holes his very first day on the course.

Howard told me, "He came home and said, 'I just can't put these golf clubs down. Golf is the game I want to play, not football.' "

Howard said, "Hal has never had a lesson from a real teaching pro. There's a nine-hole course near our house where he plays, and the fellow in charge over there told Hal, 'Just tee it up and swing big.' But I want my boy to be taught more than that. I've told Hal that if he wants to be a golfer, I want him playing and practicing eight hours a day. That's what he's been doing, and he's won the state junior and is shooting in the 70s. I would like for you to take a look at him."

I told Howard that it was a long trip from Louisiana, and I wouldn't promise I could help the boy. I suggested they go to a teacher closer to home.

But a few days later, Howard Sutton called back.

"We're on our way to Austin," he said. "I would appreciate it if you would see us."

They arrived in their own airplane and drove out to Austin Country Club near Riverside Drive. I shook hands with them in the shop, and we talked for a few minutes. Hal was a husky, handsome boy who looked strong and athletic.

"Let's go hit a few," I said.

The three of us started toward the door. I stopped.

"Mr. Sutton, if you don't mind, I'd rather you wait here," I said. "Hal and I will be back in a little while."

The first thing I did on the practice range was ask Hal to remove his golf glove so I could see how his hands fit on the club.

I watched young Hal hit balls with nearly every club in his bag. He was a powerful kid who loved to bang his driver out there a long way. But he had the touch for the shorter shots, too. It was obvious to me that Hal had a world of potential. Potential can be an anchor around your neck unless you keep it in perspective.

After maybe an hour, I asked Hal to come sit beside me in my golf cart.

"What do you think?" he said.

I said, "Here's what I would like for you to do, son. Hit your 7-iron on the practice tee more than any other full swing club. Hit your driver four times at a practice session, and then put it away. You're a good, powerful driver. I wouldn't want to see you out on the practice range wasting all those good drives that you will need on the golf course. There are golfers out here all the time throwing away their best drives on the practice range."

I knew he wouldn't like my advice about leaving his driver in his bag at practice, because I could see how he loved hitting those boomers. But he listened to me, and he nodded.

"After you hit each shot, I want your elbows pointing at the target," I said. "If you finish your swing with your right elbow pointing at the target, it will be a good shot.

"Hal," I said, "people are going to tell you your grip is too strong. They don't know what they are talking about. Ignore them. Also, people are going to say your swing is too compact. They're wrong about that, too. Your swing is just fine. Physically, you have everything it takes to be a good player. There's nothing more I can tell you, except before long you will be shooting some very low scores."

We went back to the golf shop, where Howard was waiting.

"Well?" he said.

I said, "Mr. Sutton, I have only one piece of advice for you. Don't let anybody mess with your son's swing."

In what seemed to me a very short time, I began to see Hal Sutton's name in the sports pages with regularity. He won the Western Amateur back to back, as only Chick Evans had ever done before. Hal won the National Amateur. He turned pro and won the Tournament Players championship and the National PGA and was leading money winner one year. He had found in Jimmy Ballard a teacher whose style is very close to the natural swing Hal had showed me.

After a while I realized I wasn't seeing Hal's name at the top of the sports pages anymore. I heard that he had been going to one teacher after another, changing his swing to suit each one, allowing himself to become confused about things that he never even thought about when he was playing his best.

I don't know how old Hal is by now. But I know that he is still young enough and good enough that if he puts his mind to it, and finds his own swing, he will be winning golf tournaments again.

Match Play

MATCH PLAY IS the heart and soul of amateur golf. Medal play is for the pros. There is an outstanding exception, called the Ryder Cup, when the pros root like college boys for their teammates in match play. And there are countless amateur medal tournaments. But at my club, when our members play their regular contests against each other, I almost never hear of wagers being decided by counting each stroke and adding them all up.

Members nearly always play skins (we used to call them syndicates), Nassaus, Robins, Wolf, all sorts of games that involve match play.

If a foursome of high handicappers tried to decide the winners of the wagers by obeying all the rules and counting all the strokes on a windy day at Austin Country Club, they'd better have at least one CPA in the group.

High handicappers can have a wonderful time at match play. If you are out of the hole, you pick up your ball and say "Press" and go to the next tee. You don't make everyone on the course wait while you chop it out of the trees and sink your putt for a 12.

During my thirty-three years as golf coach at the University of Texas, we played matches against the other schools in the Southwest Conference to settle the team championship.

We did have a 72-hole medal tournament at the end of the season, but it was to decide the individual champion.

College golf was much more of an amateur game in those days. Boys didn't try out for my teams so they could get training to go on the tour.

Today the colleges play medal tournaments because most of the best players want to turn pro eventually, and stroke play is the best training for what they will face.

I recall college golf as having been a special sort of fun all season when I was coaching. We would look forward eagerly to hearing how the number-one player for Rice did against the number-one for TCU in a match, for example. Rivalries may be more intense now because of the future money involved, but our rivalries got very personal.

Some say that in match play you should ignore your opponent and do your best to shoot a good score on the golf course. I always taught the opposite. My boys played against their opponents, not against the golf course. It didn't matter how many strokes you took on the hole, just so long as it was one fewer than the other fellow.

The pro is far smarter than the amateur at knowing when and how to take chances in a stroke-play tournament. An amateur in medal play might try an all-but-impossible shot and lose five strokes when it fails. A good pro will know how to make a par or bogey from the same place the amateur writes down a 10.

But in match play the amateur gauges his risks by how his opponent is faring. The amateur is better able to handle the thinking that goes with being 1-down than the thinking that goes with being one shot behind the leader.

Some people are cut out for match play. I brag about Ed White and Morris Williams, Jr., and undefeated Kirby Attwell, and many others, but one of my favorites was Ed Hopkins. If Ed needed to hit a ball two hundred yards

71

through an area the size of Helen's kitchen window to win a match, Ed believed he could do it.

At the National Intercollegiate at Pebble Beach, Ed was 7-down at the turn, and had gotten back to even on the eighteenth tee. Trying to cut the left edge of the fairway so he could go for the green in two, Ed hooked his drive into the ocean and lost the match. But he didn't lose for lack of confidence.

Other than exhibitions, I never played in a match-play tournament as a professional. I lack a quality that it takes to be good at match play. Some call it the killer instinct. I love to compete, but I never threw a fit or went into a depression if I lost a match.

A medal tournament was different. I always felt I should have done better.

Bucket Head

———

JOE BOB GOLDEN, one of my college players, brought his daughter Kate to me for her first lesson at the age of twelve.

When they arrived, I was on the range shagging balls, wearing a wire bucket upside down on my head for protection, like a football helmet.

Joe Bob told me Kate said, "That couldn't be the great teacher you've been telling me about? That man with a bucket on his head?"

Her reaction was common among new pupils who hadn't seen me picking up the practice balls as a regular thing. While I was down range, some of my club members kept practicing, so I needed a covering for my head that I could breathe through. The wire ball bucket was just the right thing.

People used to ask me why I sometimes picked up the range balls by myself. Even after we got a tractor to pick up balls, I would often drive the tractor. The reason is too simple for many people to understand. I picked up range balls because I liked doing it.

By the time I had finished, Kate had been hitting balls for at least fifteen minutes, and I had been watching her out of the corner of my bucket, so as not to make her feel self-conscious.

I told Kate a few stories about her dad and then watched her hit several different clubs.

"Kate," I said, "you're young and you have a lot of talent. People are going to be running to you constantly to tell you how you should swing. They probably really do want to help you, but don't listen to them. You and I are going to take this slowly. A little bit at a time."

Kate came to me for lessons for sixteen years.

Once while she was at the university, Kate started having terrible problems with that ugly sideways shot that I prefer to call a lateral. Knowing her father as well as I do, I figured it was hereditary.

Kate came to the club and found a place on the range.

She looked a little frightened. Those lateral shots will scare anybody.

I was walking with the aid of a cane in those days. I could still get around all right, but I needed the cane for balance and to take some of the pressure off my back.

I put the tip of my cane about an inch and a half away from her ball and leaned on the cane.

I said, "Hit that ball, Kate. You wouldn't knock an old man over, would you?"

"I'm too nervous," she said. "What if I hit you? That would be awful!"

"It sure would," I said. "So please don't hit me. Hit the golf ball."

Kate pulled herself together and hit a fine straight ball.

She's a golf pro now, and she tells me that any time the laterals attack her, she simply goes to the range and thinks about not knocking over old Bucket Head with the cane, and she's cured.

Ezar the Wizard

I PLAYED A lot of golf with my old friend Joe Ezar, a wizard with a club in his hands. As a trick shot artist, Joe rated with Joe Kirkwood and Paul Hahn as the best. Ezar was a Texan, born in Waco, and he had the wanderlust. He was known all over the world for golfing skills that were mighty close to incredible.

Fans were always asking Ezar and Kirkwood and Hahn why they didn't win every tournament they entered. All three gave the same answer: "Because every shot in a tournament is not a trick shot. Hitting the ball straight is the hardest shot of all."

Ezar would take off for South America or for Europe without a dime in his pocket. He knew his uncanny ability to handle a golf club would be his ticket. Joe would stow away on an ocean liner, and when the ship was too far from shore to make him swim, he would introduce himself all around and begin doing his tricks on the deck. By the time the ship reached port, Joe would have a lot of new friends and a nice bankroll. His new friends would discover that he was nearly as good at cards as he was at hitting a golf ball. George Low used to say Joe Ezar was the real Titanic Thompson. I've played golf with both, and I wouldn't know which way to bet between them.

One summer during the Great Depression, Joe hopped a ship to Europe to do his shows and play in a few tournaments. What he did at the Italian Open that year became the talk of the golfing world.

Joe was competing in the tournament. In those times, they played thirty-six holes a day for two days. Joe was hired to do an exhibition of trick shots the evening before the final two rounds. As always, Joe drew a big crowd.

After his routine had astounded the audience, Joe went to the putting green. He dropped three balls on a slope about twenty feet above the hole. Joe told the crowd he would sink one of the three. He sank the third. Then he went to the downhill side of the hole, dropped the three balls twenty feet from the cup, and announced that he would sink the third putt.

Joe did it.

One of the onlookers was Henry Cotton, who had shot two 67s to set a course record and lead the tournament.

Within Cotton's hearing, someone told Joe it was a wonder the Texas boy didn't hold the course record, since he could hit such marvelous shots.

Joe asked the club president, who was the boss of the tournament, how much a 66 would be worth. The president said he would pay Joe $100. Joe began to bargain.

Finally Joe said, "I'll do a 64 for $500."

Furthermore, Joe took a cigarette case from the president's pocket. On the inside of the case, Joe wrote down the scores he would shoot hole by hole to make his 64.

The next day Joe was followed by the tournament's biggest gallery. He came to the ninth hole needing a 3 for a 32. He was fifty yards from the cup in 2. Joe called the crowd's attention to his problem—and then he holed it out!

Joe shot another 32 on the second nine for his course record of 64. The president pulled out his cigarette case and read the numbers. Joe had done his record in the exact order he wrote down.

Henry Cotton said it was one of the most amazing occurrences he had ever heard of in golf. I would certainly second that opinion. Joe's 64 passed every player in the Italian Open field except Cotton, who won first money with a final 66.

Golf was Joe Ezar's means of seeing the world and standing people on their ears a long way from Wichita Falls.

The Boy from Missouri

WHEN WE WERE sitting around talking about golf and life at tournaments or teaching seminars, my old friend and colleague Horton Smith used to tell this story on himself.

In 1928, Horton won eleven tournaments on the winter tour. He was a twenty-year-old blonde-haired boy from Missouri, and suddenly everybody who paid attention to golf was saying he had become the biggest star in the game. Horton played so fast and seemingly so casually—he would just walk up to his ball and hit it, even if it happened to be the shot that would win the tournament—that onlookers were drawn in by his style.

This was during Prohibition, a year before the big Wall Street Crash, and the country club folks back East were living high. They were drinking bootleg whiskey, and the sophisticated women had started smoking cigarettes, and each club would put on a party for the professionals who came to play in their tournaments.

All the women wanted to sit beside Horton. He was a shy boy, a quiet sort like me, but he tried his best to keep up with the conversation at dinner.

One night a society woman was shining up to Horton. She offered him a cigarette.

"No, thank you. I don't smoke," Horton said.

The woman produced her flask from her purse and started to pour a glass of booze for Horton.

"No, thank you," he said. "I don't drink."

Everybody at the table was watching curiously by this time.

The woman said, "Don't you have any vices at all?"

Horton thought it over.

"Yes, ma'am," he said. "I've been tending to leave my lag putts a little too short."

Practice? What's That?

MY MEMBERS COME home from playing golf in England and Scotland for the first time, and they usually remark to me how odd it is to visit the old courses like Royal Musselburgh and Prestwick and North Berwick, and find no practice grounds.

"We change our shoes in the parking lot, and then we go straight to the tee, unless there's time to use the putting green," they say. "But there's nowhere to loosen up the grease. Why didn't those designers of those famous old courses mark off some ground where you can hit practice balls before you play?"

There are two good reasons—the balls and the clubs.

Those old courses were laid in the earth long before the modern golf ball and the steel-shafted club.

Even after the gutta perchas and other handmade balls were replaced by mass-produced balls that were more regular in performance, the golf clubs still had hickory shafts.

If you went to a practice ground and hit fifty balls with your hickory-shafted mashie, you would have to take your club back to your pro and hope he could bend and shave and hammer your shaft back into playing condition.

Until the sturdy steel shaft, golfers didn't practice. Oh, you might sneak off to an empty fairway and whack a few. But there was none of this five hundred practice balls a day that later became the routine for champions like Ben Hogan.

There's one thing, however, they still do practice at those old Scottish and English courses. They practice putting. On summer evenings when it stays light until an hour or two before midnight, whole families turn out for putting on the green in the town square.

Jess Kept Playing

JESS ROOT WAS a very wealthy member who showed up at our club every day at noon to play golf. Jess said in his opinion anyone who couldn't get free for the afternoon was misusing his life. Jess used to say, "If you can't break 80 you've got no business on the golf course. If you can break 80, you've probably got no business." But Jess was a good player who made a fortune in cotton.

In his later years Jess got into a routine in which five days a week he would take a lesson from Tinsley and then play nine holes.

He was a tall, distinguished-looking man, and you could see him frequently setting off alone, just Jess and his caddie, on the daily rounds.

As he grew still older, Jess continued taking lessons from Tinsley, but he cut his regimen down to seven holes a day.

More years went by. Jess trimmed his daily play back to four holes. He would do the twelfth, a par 3 whose tee was right outside Helen's kitchen window, and then he would play the seventeenth and eighteenth and finish at the clubhouse.

At the age of ninety-four, Jess still played golf every day. But now he would make only one hole—the long, par-5 eleventh—before he was driven home.

Jess had become quite a friend of Henry Cotton in his younger days. Jess spent a lot of time in South America on business. One year he met his friend Henry Cotton at Mar Del Plata, a fancy club outside Buenos Aires, for a golfing holiday. It was a holiday for Jess, anyhow. Cotton was a professional. He was winning money, as pros are supposed to do.

After a round, Jess took the 6-iron out of Cotton's bag and was walking around with it, talking about how good it felt, saying he was going to get himself one as much like it as could be fashioned by the manufacturer's top craftsmen.

And somehow, that evening, Jess lost the golf club. Either he forgot where he left it, or it was stolen. At any rate, the 6-iron was gone.

Cotton was aghast when Jess told him the news.

"My 6-iron! You've lost my favorite club!" Cotton cried.

"I'm sorry. I swear I'll get them to make you another."

"Impossible," Cotton said. "There will never be another 6-iron with the feel of that one. The club is irreplaceable."

Jess said that from Cotton's frosty tone, he knew their friendship was over.

Counting Greens

———

I'VE HAD MANY pupils and college players who, when asked how they had been playing, would answer, "I hit fourteen greens in regulation yesterday."

"Yes, but what did you shoot?" I would ask.

"Oh, well, I shot a 76. But that's just because the putter isn't working. From tee to green, I'm playing really good."

This idea of dividing golf into two games—striking the ball as one, and putting as the other—used to appeal to Jimmy Demaret, but it really became popular when Hogan's putter turned sour.

The sportswriters would acclaim Ben's majesty for hitting greens in regulation, but then would bemoan his faulty putting as if the act of knocking the ball into the cup was a lesser feat than knocking it onto the green in the first place.

But unless the USGA changes the rules, every stroke from tee to cup will continue to count the same. The drive, the approach and the putt are all part of the game. When you add up your scorecard, the winner will be the player with the smallest number, and that may well not be the one who hit the most greens in regulation.

Cotton on the Steel Shaft

MY SON, TINSLEY, grew up on golf courses and has been head professional at Austin Country Club for nearly twenty-five years. He knows as much about the golf swing as anyone I can think of. When he was a child, we used to look at the illustrations in Seymour Dunne's golf book together and compare swings of the great players of that era.

I remember the afternoon young Tinsley came running into the golf shop with a book under his arm. I thought it might be his homework from school.

"You're going to love this book, Daddy," he said.

I'm not much of a bookish fellow. But Tinsley was so excited that I asked him to hold up the book and let me see what it was. Then the excitement grew on me, too.

The book was *This Game of Golf,* written by one of my favorites, Henry Cotton. The book was published in London in 1948, and this was fresh off the press. I have long ago forgotten how Tinsley came by the book, but I suspect his source must have been someone in the Root family, club members who were friends with Cotton.

Not only did Cotton win the British Open three times—it was said he drove the ball so straight off the tee that there were arguments in the galleries over whether his ball was on the left side of the fairway or the right—

he had an acute understanding of the game and of the swing that many champions lack.

I read half of Cotton's book the first day Tinsley showed it to me, and then finished it within a week. Over the years, I've often asked Tinsley to lift the book out of his collection and let me borrow it for a few days. I have spent many an evening consulting with Cotton on the printed page, and for a time during his visits to the United States and his swing through the South. Henry was a popular star, played golf with Bob Hope and Bing Crosby as well as with royalty and all the famous players of his time.

I was never close to Cotton as a player, but when he became a teacher I found that we were quite a bit alike. Neither of us was a system teacher. We preferred the Vardon grip and the natural stance. We admitted the power and glory of the shut-face swinging champions, but we agreed we would rather see the clubhead more open than shut at the top of the backswing. We both had enormously strong hands and wrists—me from buffing clubs in the golf shop since I was a boy, Cotton from deliberate strength training—and naturally we liked to use our hands and wrists in the golf swing. We believed our pupils were individuals, and we treated them as such. Not least, I suppose, Cotton and I dressed like gents. I knew I would never be a guest at the fancy places in England and Scotland and Europe where Cotton was a hero, but I was dressed for it, anyhow.

Cotton and I, being about the same age, went through the great revolution together. I mean the movement of golf from hickory shafts that were handmade, to steel shafts that were produced for the millions.

This is what Cotton said in 1948 about that transition to the steel shaft from the viewpoint of a champion:

When a drive of 200 yards was considered long, it was important to save every yard, and so, some thirty years ago, much more attention was given to the playing of sliced and hooked shots, and to high and low shots, than is given today. Although every effort has been made in this country to keep golf as it was years ago, the fast-flying resilient modern ball and the steel shaft have come to control the game, and yards are cheap.

Today, given favorable yet normal conditions, drives up to 300 yards are common, and so for all intents and purposes this 50 per cent increase in length has made it unnecessary to steal those few extra yards by using the wind; the player of today, unless playing in a gale, takes the appropriate club and hits a shot, doing his best to strike the ball truly and to gauge the wind.

I do not mean that the player of today cannot play all the shots; he can—and can play them as well as they have ever been played—but he does not require them, and so counts them as superfluous, almost as trick shots.

This outlook on these shots, by the modern player, is only natural; the ball, now scientifically made and tested, can be counted on to fly dead straight if hit correctly and, unless the wind blows at gale force, a truly struck ball will hold its line with very little drift.

There is still a section of golfers who agitate for the return of the days when golf required "art and skill" as they call it, but unless we return to a ball which does not travel more than 200 yards, I fail to see how these days can ever return. Were such a thing to happen, golfers now so used to scoring relatively low would not like their scores to mount and would practice harder to improve even more on their chipping and putting.

The handicap player would be the one to suffer, for

he would feel, as did this class of player years ago, that golf was too difficult a game. Making the game more difficult will not popularize golf—this has been found in America, where golf thrives—but we must avoid the extremes and keep a happy medium.

As for this slicing and hooking so clearly marked down as being a part of the game thirty years ago: one famous player stated that he changed his stance, getting his right foot advanced, his left foot pulled back (this makes a very open stance) and the ball more forward, and then he pulled his arms across the ball. This is the surest way to slice and the one universally used, but his remarks on the hook, in which he explained that the same swing is used, but with the wrists rolled over rapidly on coming to the ball, are not very satisfying. Shades of hook and slice are more difficult to control with the present ball than with the old, unresponsive one, for any error or exaggeration is magnified; the long straight drivers today have to be very accurate strikers. . . .

Judging by the photographs and the descriptions of the old masters of this part of the game, I feel sure that the slower-flying ball would stick to the clubface longer, and so shades of hook and slice could be "worked" on to the ball by all players having good hand and wrist work.

Thirty odd years ago the best players were only asked to beat the rest, and this they did by scoring from, say, 74 to 80 on an average; today, because of the improvement in clubs, balls, the condition of the courses, and the extra competition, the best players are asked to score, say, 65 to 72 to win. But I see no reason at all why these present scores should be good enough to win in another thirty years, as you cannot stop progress.

The steel shaft has appeared in various forms in its short legal life—from the medium to the whippy, and now back to the stiff types—so fashion has dictated. All sorts and types of shafts have been invented, with the whip placed in various sections (such as by the neck of the club, up under the grip, in the middle); but the graded shaft with the various little steps in it—True Temper by name—has stood the test of years, and is still the best.

Today, 1948, there is a tendency amongst the world's star players to go for a very stiff shaft, which must also be as light as possible—i.e. strength without weight. This is a vogue only; the medium whippy shaft must be best for the average golfer.

Americans favor a chromium-plated shaft, Britons a covered shaft in a dark enamel. Steel shafts, compared with hickory, are everlasting, but just as the springs of motorcars get tired, so does the steel in the golf shaft. That is one reason the crack golfer never minds how often he changes his clubs. Some shafts play out and improve, but if they can play out a little after a time, they can play out a lot—even too much eventually.

———

It has been more than forty years since Cotton shared those ideas with us, and I would like to add one thing—a resounding hurrah for the steel shaft. Without it, golf would still be a game played only by the wealthy and the obsessive.

For years I was on the staff of Kenneth Smith, a very high-class, expensive and popular maker of clubs. I thought much of our success came because the shafts on our custom-fitted irons were a little more flexible than the labels might lead you to believe, and our lofts were a little higher.

Short Game Touch

AFTER WATCHING A pupil blade three or four chip shots clear across the back of the green from a yard in the front fringe, and then leave the next shot about six inches past his left foot, I remarked, "Well, I see one thing I am mighty happy about."

"What's that?" the pupil said.

"I'm happy you are not repairing my watch today."

Touch—which is knowing how far and how hard to hit the ball—can be learned by all but an unfortunate few. Sometimes those who at first seem to have no touch at all turn out to be the victims not of inability, but of a lack of mindfulness to the moment.

I say touch can be learned. I don't say touch can be taught.

The way you learn touch is by practice. There is no other way. I have seen players who are born with a natural sense of touch and can lay their chip shots dead as if it's the simplest thing in the world. But there are fewer of these than there are of unfortunates who have no inner guidance whatsoever.

In the great middle range of players, the best scorers will turn out to be those who consistently get into the cup in two, no more than three, strokes from about fifty yards or less from the green.

You can hook a drive into the tall grass and then turn it into a par if you will dig it out with a lofted club and follow with a good pitch or chip and putt. But if you muff a pitch or a chip, you have lost a stroke nearly every time.

Practice your pitches, chips and long lag putts. Pay attention to what you are doing. Make note of how far back you took the club to hit the shot that made the ball fly a certain distance. Take the club back to the same place and do it again. Be sure it is no fluke. Believe in it. On days when your touch is poor, you can still remember a technical thing—such as how far the ball will fly when you take your wedge back waist high—and put it to use to make a decent shot, even though you feel like a total stranger to the game.

Put variety into your practice to keep your mind on it. You might stand at the cup and lob a golf ball underhanded as far as you can. Where the ball stops, that becomes your practice distance. Using a golf club, feel you are throwing the ball back to the hole. Then lob the ball in another direction down the fairway, and begin again.

A few of these sessions will cut half a dozen strokes off your score.

So Use a Broom

SINCE MY *Little Red Book* appeared a few years ago with one of my favorite pieces of advice for golf learning— swinging a weed cutter—I have received a great many letters and phone calls from folks who ask, "What is a weed cutter? Where can I find one?"

In my younger days nearly every home had a weed cutter in the garage or barn. It is a device with a wooden handle on top and a blade on bottom, and it is swung to cut weeds or high grass.

The action of swinging a weed cutter is the same as that of swinging a golf club in the correct way.

I have asked friends to scout hardware stores for me, and I find that weed cutters are, indeed, difficult to find. With the poison that is poured into the ground to kill weeds and with the machinery that is used to mow high grass, I suppose there is not so much need for weed cutters anymore.

The good news for golfers is that you can do very much the same thing with a broom, and hardware stores still sell brooms.

Let us suppose you want to take a golf stance and brush a dandelion on the grass with a broom. You would start naturally with a slight forward press to get yourself into motion and then you would take the broom back without rolling your wrists open.

Brushing through the dandelion, your broom head would be square. It would look silly to you if the broom head was open or closed.

You probably have a broom in a closet somewhere at home. Go get it and make a few gentle brushes on the carpet, pretending the broom is a golf club. Notice how ridiculous it feels if you roll your wrists open to the right on your backswing when you know your purpose is to bring the broom down square to your spot on the rug. It's the same with a golf club, except the correct action is more likely to escape your detection with the lighter instrument.

When I tell pupils to "brush the grass," some think I mean they should skim the grass with their clubface. For the average player, skimming the grass produces a thin hit. Instead, think of brushing the grass off your sidewalk after a mowing, holding the broom with your golf grip. The wrist action is the same as in a good swing.

The weed cutter is still my favorite learning tool, but if you can't find one, use a broom.

The Right Way
to Waggle

SOME GREAT PLAYERS never waggle before they swing. Horton Smith used to walk up to the ball, plant his feet, put the clubhead on the ground and with a small forward press launch the swing that won him many championships.

But I like a waggle to start my engine, so long as it follows two rules:

First, your waggle must be simply a loosening of tension and a turning of the key in your ignition, with no ritual for you to worry about. As Ben Hogan said, "Don't groove your waggle." I have seen pupils concentrate so intensely on their waggle that they become tense, which is just the opposite of the reason for waggling in the first place.

Second, your waggle is a rehearsal of the beginning of your swing, so you must avoid rolling your wrists open while you are waggling. You want your clubface looking at the ball for the first few inches, not looking at the sky.

Some of the top teachers and players say the waggle should go backward and then come forward until your clubhead passes the ball. This is a good way to complete the rehearsal aspect of the waggle, and it might work well for you, but to me it is not essential.

One thing I do like when I waggle, though, is to feel my feet, maybe my toes moving inside my shoes, getting a grip on the earth, settling into a steady platform that is lively and ready for the weight shift.

Footwork is a vital part of the swing, and you should make yourself aware of the earth under your feet during your waggle.

The waggle is not just to prepare for a swing of the hands and arms or a swing from above the waist. It is to prepare to set the entire swing in motion. A good golf swing uses every muscle in the body and produces an exhilarating feeling like no other I know.

Learning Young

I HAVE ALWAYS believed a youngster should start playing golf when he or she really wants to, rather than being forced into it by a parent. But I concede that many kids wouldn't know whether they wanted to play golf or not unless they were exposed to it by a parent or an older sibling, or unless they were lucky enough to grow up near a golf course.

It's a good idea to give a small child a toy club to fool

around with or a cut-down real club, as long as it is not so heavy it will ruin the child's natural grip. Encouraging a child to hit putts at a very early age is always a wonderful thing to do, as this will start teaching the most important part of the game at an impressionable stage.

Once you see the child does want to play golf, I strongly advise you take the child to see a pro, not for a steady program of lessons but to guide the child's learning.

With all the junior golf schools and tournaments available today—and the golf on television to show swings to mimic—it is possible for a child to become a seasoned player by the age of twelve.

Learning the game young can pay off far down the line.

If a pupil comes to me at age forty and wants to learn golf starting from the very beginning, it is a difficult process, because almost everything I say sounds unnatural.

But a forty-year-old pupil who may not have played golf in twenty-five years can advance quickly if that pupil learned the swing fundamentals at a young age.

I had a pupil at Cherry Hills one summer who was about forty and was finding the principles of golf impossible to grasp. A visitor from Mexico City walked up to say hello, and the two began speaking fluent Spanish.

"How did a Denver banker learn to speak Spanish so well?" I asked my pupil later.

"I was very lucky," he said. "I went to an elementary school where they started teaching us Spanish in the first grade. I had Spanish classes for two hours a week until the sixth grade. After that, I never studied Spanish again, but I have retained the language. If I spend a week or two in Mexico, I get so good at it that people think I'm a native."

Nothing beats learning young.

Advising Kirby

WHEN KIRBY ATTWELL came out for the golf team at the University of Texas, I told him, "Son, if we can take just one stroke per year off of your game, you will be a top-notch player by the time you graduate."

I didn't need to be Einstein to figure that out. Kirby was shooting a steady 73 or 74 as a freshman.

In three years on the varsity, Kirby won every match he played.

After he received his diploma, Kirby asked if I thought he should turn pro.

I said, "Kirby, you're a top-notch player, all right, but I honestly think you should strive to be the best amateur player you can be in whatever business you pursue."

In those days—the middle 1950s—a professional tournament purse was about ten thousand dollars. Jack Burke, Jr., won four tournaments in a row and picked up only eight thousand dollars in prize money. There were maybe six head pro country club jobs in the country that paid as much as twenty-five thousand dollars per year.

Just a few years after Kirby graduated, golf was changed radically by two things—the arrival of the electric golf cart and the appearance about the same time of Arnold Palmer.

When Palmer would hitch up his pants and march down the fairway, the crowds would go crazy. Television began to show more tournaments because of him, and he attracted millions of people to the game of golf, where most of them started riding electric carts. The club pro got a piece of the cart rental, and salaries went up all around the golf world.

If Kirby had come along about ten years later than he did, he would have been a success on the tour.

Instead he became a successful businessman in Houston and club champion at River Oaks.

When he comes to see me now, we sometimes talk about what might have been. I know he will always wonder if he could have become a winner as a touring pro. I believe in Kirby's case, it was just a matter of timing.

Helen, the Recruiter

PRESTON MOORE WAS a fine high school player in Houston, son of a Houston city golf champion who was killed in the Navy in World War II. I knew Preston's father, and I also knew the Moores were a family of Princetonians. It was preordained that Preston would go to Princeton, so I never gave a thought to his joining my golf team at the University of Texas.

The summer of Preston's senior year in high school, he was playing in a state junior tournament at Austin Country Club. My wife, Helen, was the official scorer who walked along with Preston's group.

Helen hadn't known Preston before, but watching him play golf and talking to him on the course, she liked the young man quite a lot.

I'm not sure if Preston knew anything about me, but he had become very fond of the pretty woman who was scoring for his group.

Preston went home and told his mother he had decided to go to Texas. I believe it set off a considerable family debate. Finally Preston's mother told him he must apply at Princeton. "If you are accepted at Princeton, then you can go to any college you want," she said, probably believing nobody, especially a Moore, would turn down Princeton to spend four years in Austin.

But as Preston told me later, he kept thinking about the nice woman who had asked him to come to Texas, and after turning the decision over in his mind and heart, he drove to Austin and enrolled.

When I heard about it, I remarked to Helen over the dinner table that I was proud this boy from Houston had decided to play for my team instead of for Princeton.

"Oh, I'm so glad," she said. "Somehow, I knew he would."

"How do you know about it?" I asked, surprised.

"Why, Harvey, I asked him to come here," she said. "He's such a nice boy, I just knew he would love it here."

After graduating from Texas, Preston served as an officer in the Air Force and later attended Harvard Business School and became Assistant Secretary of Commerce under President Bush. He still plays a good game of golf, but his main sport is running marathons.

I enjoy Preston's friendship, and I never would have known him if not for Helen, the recruiter.

I gave Preston's son his first golf lesson at age seven. Preston brought the boy up to Austin Country Club from Houston.

The boy walked onto the range carrying his clubs in a little canvas bag slung under his right arm instead of across his back.

95

I told him, "Son, the first important thing for you to learn is the right way to carry your clubs. We don't want to give your opponents too much confidence."

Yoga

A FEW OF my senior friends, seasoned players, have taken up the study of yoga, which is a practice that teaches complete and intense concentration of the mind, as well as artful, healthy stretching of the muscles and especially strengthening of the small muscles.

I can't imagine a more useful pursuit for a golfer than the study of yoga.

I believe the small muscles must combine with the big muscles to hit the ball far and straight. Look at John Daly with his huge turn and long windup. The big muscles of his back, hips and legs pour the power into his violent swing, but it is the small muscles that make the snap and precision that launch those 350-yard drives. In my opinion, Daly is the most exciting player to come along in years. If he were to study yoga to calm his mind and tune his small muscles, there is no telling how good he could be.

I heard somewhere that Greg Norman, another power hitter and a great champion, is applying himself to Zen and to the martial arts to build his power of concentration.

In Zen they ask what is the sound of one hand clapping. Well, what you hear from me is the sound of two hands clapping at the idea of golfers delving into these ancient disciplines.

All seasoned players know, or at least have felt, that when you are playing your best, you are much the same as in a state of meditation. You are free of tension and chatter. You are concentrating on one thing. It is the ideal condition for good golf.

One of my longtime pupils told me recently that he meditates at the club. "I do it in the evenings on the practice range, hitting balls. It utterly calms my mind and leaves me refreshed," he said. "No telling how much hitting golf balls has saved me in psychiatrist bills."

I have always taught that golf requires the kind of muscles that snap a whip rather than the kind of muscles that pick up a heavy barbell.

Except for the famous amateur Frank Stranahan, and a few others over the years, weightlifting has been frowned upon by the better players.

Now weightlifting has become acceptable and even encouraged. There is a trailer van that follows the pro tour carrying weightlifting machines and dead weights.

I suppose any exercise that strengthens the forearms and hands is probably good, as would be a turning exercise that builds muscles in the middle of the body.

Anything that strengthens your hips and legs is good, too.

In my mind, the best exercise is to swing a heavy practice club every day. I know swinging the heavy club builds the right muscles for golf.

Yoga is also the study of breathing. As I grow older, I reflect on how we take breathing for granted. Proper deep breathing is a joy, it makes you feel good, it calms your mind. Deep breathing is wonderful on the golf course as a provider of oxygen and strength throughout your body. I'll bet on a deep breather any time over a player who just breathes to stay alive.

With the stretching exercises that yoga teaches, you gain flexibility. If your body is flexible, you can keep playing good golf for your entire life.

I Wonder Why

———

THE GOOD PLAYERS are almost always the ones who ask me to watch them on the putting green. The high handicappers, who need it the most, had rather do anything than have a putting lesson.

Pick It Up

———

WHEN YOUR OPPONENTS concede you a gimme putt, you should show the courtesy to pick up your ball and walk away. There's always the player who says, "Aw, I'll just putt it for fun, anyway," and then misses and says, "That was only for practice."

They may not write it on the scorecard, but everybody

knows down deep that the missed putt should have counted, and maybe they shouldn't concede any more to this player.

The Great One's Tricks

———

HARRY VARDON HAD a habit of touching his right toe to the spot where his ball had been before his swing had sent it somewhere else.

After his follow-through, the great champion would look back down to the spot and touch it before he walked on.

I believe this was a well-thought-out piece of his technique. He was always reminding himself that the point of the swing is to hit a spot.

Vardon also carried a piece of chalk. He rubbed the chalk on the face of his club before he hit each shot. It was said he did it to help get backspin, but I believe Vardon was reminding himself to hit the ball on the chalk—the clubface.

He was a master. He knew you must hit what you swing at.

Impact Drills

JAMES BRAID USED to set up a mound of sand a foot in front of the ball and tell his pupils to knock it down with their follow-through. Copying him, I did the same now and then at the first Austin Country Club at Hancock Park when I was a young pro.

Then someone thought of the idea of whacking an old auto tire with an old golf club. For years it was popular practice to slam a tire with a club until you had knocked the rubber twenty feet or more.

This is a very good drill for improving your clubhead speed and getting the feeling of a solid hit, but I know of too many players who have injured their wrists and elbows while bashing away at auto tires.

The so-called impact bags that are in use today by many teachers are better than auto tires because they are plastic bags filled with rags and thus softer.

You still must be careful not to swing too hard at an impact bag, because you can hurt yourself.

Other than the danger, another reason I don't use the impact bag is that there is no follow-through at the end of the swing.

Try a Little Closer

IF YOUR MIDDLE irons get off and you can't figure out why, try standing a little closer to the ball.

Reaching out too much for the ball causes a loss of balance with consequences that wind up in the bunker.

Moe Norman, the amazing Canadian, reaches way out for the ball and hits it straight as a rifle shot, but I don't see any of the world's great players copying his style.

Remember that with your back angled forward, your arms should hang pretty much straight down, as though you are carrying something with both hands.

I believe I have never seen a good golfer who stands too close to the ball. If you really are too close, your instinct will tell you that you can't swing at it.

Don January stands so close to the ball that sometimes it looks as if he might hit himself on the foot. But Don has been a winner for more than fifty years.

A Grip Check

SEE IF YOU can hit three shots in a row on the practice range without ever taking your hands off the handle or moving your fingers in any way.

If you can do this, your grip is solid and you can use a golf glove all summer without wearing a hole in the palm.

Reassurance

SOMETIMES WHEN I am feeling low, I remember a little poem I heard when I was a boy.

> When your time comes to
> Pass on someday
> The only things you can keep
> Are what you gave away.

Jones's Rules and One More

BOBBY JONES SAID because tension is golf's worst enemy, he had set forth six rules that would help develop a freewheeling swing.

1. Grip the club lightly, mainly in the fingers, and make sure you can feel the clubhead.
2. In addressing the ball, arrange your posture as naturally and comfortably as possible.
3. Use the legs and hips in beginning the backswing, and swing the club back rather than picking it up with the hands and arms.
4. Be sure your backswing is long enough that your downswing will have time to get up speed before contact.
5. Start your downswing in a leisurely fashion, in no hurry coming down, with the acceleration smooth and natural.
6. When it comes time to hit, don't leap at the ball, but keep on swinging until the ball has had a good start down the fairway, and the clubhead has done its job.

To these rules, I would add one more for the average golfer—be sure your shoulders are square to the line.

Luck

———

TO MY COLLEGE boys and to my other pupils who were heading into tournaments, I would always say, "Play well," instead of saying, "Good luck."

Like life, golf is a game of good breaks and bad

breaks. There is nothing fair about it. But the person who plays well usually has a larger share of good breaks. The old saying is, "The more I practice, the luckier I get."

However, luck is out of our control. We can only try our best on each shot and keep on trying until the game is over. Luck will have its own way.

After thirty-eight holes of a semifinal match at the PGA at Olympia Fields, Leo Diegel and Walter Hagen came to the third tee all square.

Diegel bashed one of his powerful shut-face drives far down the fairway. Hagen, a swayer and lunger, hit a big slice over the trees and into the deep rough. Diegel had a simple approach to the green. As Hagen waded through the high grass toward his ball, it appeared he would have no chance to reach the green from his miserable position.

But arriving at his ball, Hagen found it sitting up nice and fat atop a perfect slab of turf being grown in a nursery that supplied patches for the greens.

Diegel was shaken to his toes by the sight of Hagen's second shot flying long and high over the trees and onto the putting surface. Leo managed to halve that hole with a par, but he topped his drive on the next tee and the match was soon finished.

Yes, a player must have a certain amount of luck to win a major championship, but luck by definition is unpredictable. Don't count on luck to get you out of a tight spot. Better you do your best with each shot as it comes, and accept the luck however it falls.

A Word from the Wise

TOMMY KITE TOLD me that in a tournament one year at Harbour Town, he hit his second shot into the rear fringe of the green, a few feet beyond the putting surface.

Tommy reached back and his caddie, Mike Carrick, handed him the club he wanted to use for the chip shot, an 8-iron.

After carefully studying the chip, Tommy, who is one of the best chippers in the history of the game, drew back his club and chili-dipped the shot, moving the ball three feet.

Stunned, Tommy turned and stared at Mike.

"Well, I still believe that's the right club," Mike said.

Tommy laughed. These words of wisdom from his caddie and old friend put Tommy's mind back to the job at hand.

He took his stance again with the 8-iron and chipped the ball into the hole for a par.

Get It Close

IN A LIFETIME of playing, teaching and watching golf, I have seen very few three-putts caused by missing a second putt that is a little short of the hole.

On the other hand, I have seen countless three-putts caused by missing a second putt that is three or four feet beyond the hole.

It's usually a simple matter to rap in a ball that is just short of the hole, because you see how the putt is breaking and you already have a feel for the distance.

But the three-foot comebacker following a putt that has sped past the hole, well, this is the putt that has driven many players almost to the madhouse.

I have always told my pupils to try to let their putts die at the hole and give luck a chance. A putt that is struck too hard will spin out if it grazes the hole. But a putt that is rolling slowly will slip into the hole like a mouse.

The average golfer pays little if any attention to one of the elements that dictates the speed of a putt—the grain.

The grain is the direction in which the grass grows.

Putting against the grain is like putting uphill. If you are going down-grain and hit an up-grain putt, you are liable to knock your ball off the green. But I seldom have seen average golfers give any thought at all to the grain. They will pace off the distance and squint at the line and plumb-bob, but hardly ever do they examine the grass to see which way it grows.

I think some of the television announcers do the golfing public a disservice when, during professional tournaments, the commentators speak as though a player who leaves a medium-length putt a few inches short is lacking in courage.

The average golfer needs to realize that rolling a ten-footer up to the front edge of the cup is to be applauded, not sneered at.

The only time I can imagine when it would be dreadfully wrong to leave a putt short is if you must sink it to win the match or the tournament or the skin. Even then, you wouldn't want to show such shaky nerves that you would rap it several feet past.

The Remarkable Cherry

IN THE LATE 1940s my college boys from West Texas started telling me about a player named Don Cherry. They said he had a swing that went back about waist high, and he was beating them all. He played Billy Maxwell nine times in tournament matches on the West Texas amateur circuit, which was for years a very lively series of events that drew the best golfers to compete for prizes and for the Calcutta purses, big money. Cherry beat Maxwell eight of those times, my boys told me.

I first saw Cherry in San Antonio one year at the Texas

Open at Brackenridge Park. His swing was truly unique. It looked like Doug Sanders's swing, but shorter, and it shared one characteristic with Byron Nelson's and Dr. Cary Middlecoff's: like them, Cherry cocked his wrists on his downswing. I would never try to teach Cherry's swing to anyone, but it was simple and most effective.

Against a Texas Open field that included big hitters like Jimmy Thomson and Chick Harbert, Cherry won the long driving contest.

When I asked his opinion of Cherry as a player, Jimmy Demaret said, joking, "The reason he won't get his swing too far back is he carries his money in his right trouser pocket."

Jimmy went on to say Cherry didn't know what "out of bounds" meant, because he had only seen the fairways. "Nobody hits the ball closer to the hole than this kid. I don't care if his swing is one inch long, just so he finishes it."

Jimmy and Cherry became good friends. When Cherry started performing in night clubs as a singer, Jimmy would often be in the front row and would go to the microphone and sing a few tunes himself.

First as an amateur, then as a pro, Cherry would follow the tour for long periods and play in tournaments. He could afford to do this as an amateur because of his singing career. He would work in nightclubs in tour cities until well after midnight and arrive in fine shape for an early tee time, because he never smoked a cigarette or tasted a drink of alcohol in his life, carrying through on a promise he made his mother.

Caddies called him "Banda Gold," after one of his hit records, "Band of Gold."

Cherry had been an outstanding athlete in high school in several sports, including football. He picked up golf by caddying at Wichita Falls Country Club, home of a top amateur named Rufus King. Don taught himself his highly individual swing by playing with a wooden-shafted 5-iron on a hole he and his pals marked out in a pasture.

He played in the Masters ten times as an amateur and played on three Walker Cup teams. At the ceremony following the Walker Cup matches at the Old Course at St. Andrews one year, after Cherry had beaten British Amateur champion Joe Carr, Lord Brabazon, captain of the Royal and Ancient Society, asked Don to sing a song for the crowd of thousands gathered at the clubhouse.

Don sang, "I Believe." The newspapers reported it was this philosophy that led the United States to win the matches.

The day before this same Walker Cup began, Lord Brabazon was showing USGA Secretary Joe Dey around the course. Golf on television was a new thing then, and Dey wanted to see where all the camera cables were laid, most of them underground. Joe Dey was very particular about observing the rules of golf, and he wanted to be sure the presence of television did not strain the rules in any way.

About twenty yards behind and to the left of the eighteenth green, a piece of cable lay exposed near the steps leading into the clubhouse. Joe looked for a white line that would indicate ground under repair.

"I don't see a white line," Joe said to Lord Brabazon. "What do we do if a player hits his ball here?"

Lord Brabazon replied, "I dare say we should raise his handicap."

Thumbing It

———

IN HIS PRIME, Byron Nelson gripped his putter with his right thumb arched on top, pressing down into the grip for control.

Horton Smith and Johnny Revolta used the same style of grip. They said it helped them keep the putter blade on line through contact, and also helped their feeling for distance.

Because the act of putting is nearly entirely a matter of touch, there is no one grip that is suitable to everyone.

But like everything that is really important, putting has one fundamental that must be observed. In putting, the fundamental is to keep your head still. In life, for me, the fundamental is simply to treat others as I would wish to be treated.

Waxo's Puzzle

———

I HEARD ABOUT the lament of the Nashville sportswriter, Waxo Green, who said he could tell he was getting old because his iron clubs all carried the same distance.

This is not the fault of age. As you get older, you may expect to lose some distance with your irons, but the yardage between clubs should stay fairly constant.

The reason Waxo's irons all go the same distance is a lack of strength.

I see this among beginners, especially women, and older golfers who let their muscles get out of shape. These older golfers steadily descend to a level of not hitting the ball hard enough for the loft to make any difference. They are just clunking the ball with a hunk of steel. That's why their 4-irons go as far as their 8-irons.

It takes a hearty spank to make the ball go. The weak hand will not do it.

For anyone living with Waxo's Puzzle, I suggest stretching your muscles, doing flexibility exercises for a few minutes every day.

If you will do the stretching for five minutes in the evening and follow by swinging a weighted golf club for a short while, in a couple of weeks you will see a big change in your clubhead speed. I received a letter with a New York postmark, written on stationery from Winged Foot, that says, "Why do you keep harping on swinging a heavy club? You say it over and over. Surely with the many advances in golf technology, there must be a better way to build golf muscles other than swinging a heavy club. Swinging a heavy club is very boring."

Golf muscles are not for sale. If they were, golfers would pay almost any price. Golf muscles must be built and strengthened and then kept in tune. There are no short cuts. Swinging a heavy club is not only the best way, it is the only way that I know that succeeds for sure.

Whether you have Waxo's Puzzle or not, swinging the heavy club a few minutes every day is a certain way to hit the ball farther.

The Cookie Bakers

SOME GOLF TEACHERS are like Cookie Bakers. They use the same recipe on every pupil. Many times this technical discipline is successful, especially if the pupil is the right build and temperament and is willing to understand and to practice. But sometimes the search for the perfect formula will drive a pupil to one Cookie Baker after another, along the way losing any sense of what is consistently effective.

You must follow a plan to play consistent golf. Having no plan at all is chaos. Golfers know this, but they are always changing their plans to embrace new methods, hoping for the miraculous.

The first week Ben Hogan's classic book on fundamentals was in the stores, I could see during my duties as starter on the first tee that the book was already popular.

Many of our club members and guest players showed up with changed grips, their V's now pointing up their noses instead of toward their right shoulders.

Their drives landed in the right rough.

Following the advice in Hogan's book has turned out many fine players. His fundamentals are solid, the writing is by the great Herbert Warren Wind, and the illustrations by Tony Ravielli are as good as I can imagine being done.

This book explains the way Hogan did it. At that time nearly everybody wanted to do it like Hogan did it.

But few golfers are strong enough to play with their

V's pointing at their noses. Most golfers are fighting a slice, not a hook. Few are dedicated enough or have the time to hit hundreds of practice balls every day, as Hogan did.

The Hogan grip soon had slices bombing all over Austin Country Club.

As close as I come to baking a cookie is to say my recipe will show two or three knuckles on your left hand grip, never one or four. I like to think if there is anything that would mark a golfer as a pupil of mine, it would be that player's grip.

Observation

I AM ALWAYS interested in seeing how young players do when they first begin getting into contention in tournaments. I am less interested in whether the young ones are winning than I am in how they conduct themselves in the pressure of contention. This is where you see those who will become champions. I find pleasure in watching for future champions as much as I enjoy watching those who are already champions.

If I could talk to these young players who are just getting into position to have a chance to win, I would tell them all the same thing—be yourself, play your own game.

The Initiation

CLAUDE HARMON TOOK Jimmy Demaret's job as head pro at River Oaks when Jimmy went off to the Navy in World War II.

I knew I had been under consideration for that job. I'm glad Claude got it. River Oaks is the only place that could have tempted me to leave Austin Country Club.

I soon ran into Claude at a seminar and asked if the River Oaks job was going to his satisfaction.

He said, "I arrived at the club with forty-four dollars in my pocket and lost forty dollars playing golf with members the first day. There are some serious players at River Oaks. One of them already told me he knows far more about the swing than I do."

After River Oaks, Claude moved on to Winged Foot and Seminole. He became a famous teacher. He hired a lot of Texas boys as assistants, like Dave Marr, among others. In the late afternoons Claude would sit in the grill and talk golf, but so far as I know nobody kept notes of what Claude was saying.

I wish Claude had produced an instruction book about his shut-face swing. I don't teach that swing, and am not comfortable talking about it, but I'd like to read Claude's teachings.

The Path to Success

As a young teacher I learned never to promise anyone instant success. Instant success does come for some gifted pupils, but for the average pupils success is a journey of testing their intention.

I learned early that it was important to start with the grip. Sometimes I changed it radically at once, and sometimes gently and slowly, depending on the pupil's ability. Some grips I never changed at all, even though they might have been less than perfect. If the ball kept flying well, it might be the best grip for this pupil's swing.

There are the naturally perfect grips, too, like the beautiful grip of Ben Crenshaw, but naturals are rare.

Along with the grip, the first thing I try to give my pupils is the mind picture that will produce a good golf swing without going into technical talk.

If you have a good grip and can see the shot clearly in your mind and use the muscles picture of Clip The Tee or Brush The Grass, your swing will work—unless you start to doubt it.

She Learned
the Best Way

———

A PUPIL WAS telling me about a Dallas woman named Carolyn Harper, who was the champion at two clubs and could go around from the men's tees better than most men.

The pupil said Carolyn's husband, Wayne, was a scratch player. When they got married, Carolyn told him she wanted to learn to play golf.

"You know what he did?" my pupil asked.

"He decided to teach her himself?" I guessed.

"No," said my pupil, a woman from Dallas who was in town visiting her daughter at the university. "He did the cruelest thing."

"What? Cruel?"

"He made her spend a whole year chipping and putting before she could start taking lessons from a pro, and it was even longer before she was allowed to play a round of golf."

I don't argue with pupils. But I was impressed by the Harper family plan for learning golf. I'm sure Carolyn saw the wisdom in getting to know golf from the hole outward. Carolyn and Wayne are to be congratulated for their patient investment of time and devotion in the beginning. After she had spent a year chipping and putting, I would imagine she was shooting good scores as soon as she went out on the course.

A Motto

PLAY THE SHOT you can play best, not the shot that would look the best if you could pull it off.

Walter's Way

WHEN I PLAYED an exhibition with Walter Hagen, it appeared to me that the great man would now and then drive his ball into the trees just so he could show the fans his genius at hitting recovery shots.

Before the round ended, I decided it was more than showmanship on Hagen's part. Putting his ball in trouble kept him from getting bored. One reason Hagen loved the seaside courses of Europe was that the winds and the uneven fairways made the game more interesting for a genius who grew tired of the ordinary good lies in most American fairways. In our exhibition, I would see a sparkle come to Hagen's eye when he faced an especially challenging shot.

When I hear golfers complain about bad lies, saying the breaks are going against them, I remember Hagen, who was excited by the challenge of his ball being behind a tree in the tall grass. Hagen looked upon a difficult recovery as an opportunity to thrill himself and the fans and shake the spirit of an opponent.

I heard that a little boy stepped up to Hagen as he approached a drive that had come to rest beside a bush. "I'm sorry you keep getting such bad breaks, sir," the boy said.

"Thank you, son," Hagen replied, smiling. "But regardless of the breaks, there my ball lies, and from there I will have to play it."

Forty More Yards
for Bobby

MY SON, TINSLEY, was a member of the Future Farmers of America. One summer day in 1951 I was standing outside the clubhouse of our Riverside Drive course, watching one of Tinsley's cows eating the grass by the barn, when I became aware of a slim young man who was trying to catch my eye.

"Mr. Penick, my name is Bobby Moncrief. I want to play golf for you," he said.

"How much do you weigh?" I asked.

"One hundred and eighteen pounds," he said.

I said, "Wait here a minute."

Inside the golf shop I picked out a 7-iron and a 3-wood

off the rack. I took the clubs back outside and handed them to Bobby.

"Swing those clubs for me," I said.

"You mean go to the range?"

"No, just swing the clubs. One at a time," I said.

As Bobby swung the clubs, he told me he had played last year on the freshman team at SMU, but he wanted to go to school in Austin.

"I like this 3-wood," Bobby said, swinging it outside the golf shop. "I always hit a 3-wood off the tee in high school. Last year I finally started using a driver because I just absolutely had to have another twenty-five yards."

"How far do you hit your driver?" I asked.

"About 235 when my cleats come off the ground."

I asked if he was enchanted by distance or if he ever practiced his short game.

"Yes sir, my short game is good. I was such a short hitter off the tee in high school that I had to develop a good short game to win. My short game is accomplished."

"Never take your short game for granted," I said. "Keep practicing it above all."

He said, "Yes sir," and stood waiting.

I said, "I'd never take a boy away from SMU, but if you go to school in Austin I want you on my golf team."

I hadn't seen Bobby hit a ball, but I had seen his swing and looked into his eyes. I could see he was a player.

"There's only one thing I can give you, if you come here," I said.

"I'm not asking for anything," he said.

"I don't mean illegal inducements."

"What, then?"

I said, "I'll give you forty more yards off the tee."

Bobby made the top six the next spring in our qualifying tournament. He played with good players like Lee

119

Pinkston, Wesley Ellis, Joe Bob Golden and Fred Black-mar. Fred was the national left-hander champion and the father of Phil Blackmar, who plays on the tour.

I got busy with Bobby on the practice range. We concentrated on timing. Timing is different from rhythm and tempo. My dictionary says timing is the regulation of speed to produce the most effective result. I don't know how else to explain timing other than to say timing is hitting the ball at the right time in your swing. A swing could be rhythmic and have beautiful tempo but hit the ball at the wrong time. You see a lot of players with beautiful swings who are short hitters. They usually have poor timing. I think you are born with good timing. You see a bunch of kids in a boxing gym hitting the light bags, and you can tell which ones were born with timing and which are trying to develop it.

Bobby Moncrief was born with it.

I made him a short lecture before we began to discuss his forthcoming increase in distance. I said, "Stay under the ball and behind it. If you get out in front of the ball, you lose your power. You will find if you stay under, you will stay behind."

He knew what I meant by under. I meant swing under instead of over.

In a short time, Bob was hitting 270-yard drives. All he needed was the picture—under and behind.

When he comes to visit, he always reminds me of under and behind. That image is still his swing thought after a long run as a top amateur.

He had it made into a sign: UNDER AND BEHIND.

One year Bobby broke his favorite driver, a persimmon Wilson, in a tournament out of town. He had it rebuilt, but the new driver felt different from the one he loved.

When he returned to our club on Riverside, I walked out on the range to watch him hit his new driver.

Bobby hit four of the wildest rainbow slices I ever saw at any driving range.

"Let me have that driver," I said.

I took out my penknife, cut off the plastic band at the top of the handle, and then used the knife to peel off the grip. Underneath the leather grip was a piece of cork that covered the shaft.

"It's fixed," I said.

Bobby placed his hands on the cork, waggled a couple of times, and hit a long drive as straight as you could draw it with a ruler

I said, "Your grip was too big. Your hands are fast, and the big grip was making you leave the club behind."

Over the years Bobby has told dozens, maybe hundreds, of people that I have wizardry powers. He used the driver story as his example.

But it's not wizardry. It's my craft. When you have seen many thousands of hands gripping golf clubs for decades, and you know the swing of the player you're observing, it is a simple thing to see a grip that does not fit.

The Lesson for Today

———

I WAS WALKING across the lobby at the Red Carpet Inn on the Katy Freeway in Houston, and I ran into Bobby Moncrief, who had been out of school for quite some time.

"What brings you to Houston?" he asked.

"I'm speaking to a roomful of assistant pros in a PGA seminar this morning," I said.

"What're you going to tell them?"

I hadn't made up my mind what I was going to say to the young pros, but as I looked at Bobby Moncrief I began to get an idea.

"Bobby," I said, "you're nowhere near to being the best golfer I ever coached."

I realize this sounds like a strange thing to say to a man who beat Billy Casper and Joe Conrad in the U.S. Amateur. Bobby looked sort of surprised that I would be so blunt, but he nodded in agreement.

"And yet," I said, "of all the players I ever coached, I believe you tried the hardest. You won a lot of matches just because you tried harder than your opponent did. What I want to know is, why did you try so hard?"

Bobby thought it over.

"I guess it's very simple," he said. "Before I teed off in a match, I reminded myself how sick I was going to feel if I lost. I can't stand the sensation of anybody beating me."

I considered what he had said.

"Bobby, you've given me my topic for the seminar," I said.

"You mean try hard to win when you play golf?"

I said, "No, these are youngsters who will do a great deal of teaching. I want them to learn as teachers to feel as bad if they don't help a pupil as you feel if you lose a match. That's the kind of teacher I would like to go to, and I hope it's the kind I am."

Be Mindful

GOOD PLAYERS HAVE the power to think while they are competing. Most golfers are not thinking, even when they believe they are. They are only worrying.

Worrying is a misuse of your mind on the golf course. Whatever your obstacle, worry will only make it more difficult. Further, it is impossible to make a good golf swing if your muscles are too tense.

Rather than worrying, be mindful of the shot at hand and go ahead and play it as if you are going to hit the best shot of your life. You really might do it.

Make It a Game

RATHER THAN STAND on the practice range and hit ball after ball, I suggest you sometimes break the routine and turn your practice into a game.

You know what clubs you hit all the way around your own course. Start in your mind on the first tee. Hit your driver. Decide where that drive would leave you on the course. If you're a 5-iron away, you figure, pick up your 5-iron and hit it at a target.

If you believe your 5-iron missed the green—and you might as well be honest, because you're the only person who knows what you are doing—maybe you need your sand wedge.

You can skip the putting at this period. You'll do the putting later when you take a ball and go around the clock and count your strokes.

I recommend that you do not always prop up each iron shot or fairway wood into a good lie simply because you are on the practice tee.

There is something to say for the argument that pupils should always practice from a good lie so as to build their confidence. But I like to have my good players dump a bucket of balls onto the ground and hit them more or less as they lie, scattering them into different spots. I would insist on a clean lie only when I wanted to observe the divot.

On the golf course you do not get to scrape the ball around with your clubhead until you get a good lie. You play the ball as you find it.

I think you should practice dealing with reality on the range. Not every session, of course, but now and then you should practice hitting out of bad lies. It will make them more familiar, less daunting, on the golf course. Also, it will sharpen your concentration at practice. Supreme concentration is the peak experience of the golf swing.

Three Most
Common Faults

THE THREE MOST common faults I see among high handicappers are:

1. They aim to the right of their target.
2. They come over the top, which is a natural result of
   aiming to the right.
3. They keep their heads down too long.

Fifty More Yards
for John

JOHN TRIMBLE GREW up playing on a tight course in
Orange, Texas. The fairways were lined with trees. Feeling hemmed in, John developed a hands-and-arms
game. He aimed the ball and guided it, and he hit what
he was aiming at. He just didn't hit the ball very far.

I noticed John's name when as a high school senior he

lost to the colorful Howie Johnson, 1-up, in the finals of a tournament.

I invited him to come to Austin and see me. We played a round of golf together, both of us carrying our bags. John shot a 73 at Austin Country Club on Riverside Drive. Back at the clubhouse, I offered him an arrangement. He could sleep in Hill Hall, the athletic dorm, and eat his meals at the training table. Best of all, in John's eyes, was the news that he could play golf free at Austin Country Club for the next four years.

When John arrived for classes in the fall, I took him aside and said, "John, how would you feel about adding another fifty yards to your tee ball?"

He looked at me as if I had asked if he would like to have a million dollars.

"Coach, are you kidding me?" he said. "What's the catch?"

"There's no catch," I said. "But don't answer me right now. Think it over tonight. In the morning if you decide you want to hit the ball fifty yards farther off the tee, you come and tell me."

Early the following day, John sought me out.

"I want the fifty yards, Coach," he said.

"This will require dedication on your part. For the next three or four months, you won't be able to hit the fairway very often. But if you will commit yourself to it, you will have your fifty yards."

John said he would do whatever was necessary, and we got busy at once.

"We have to build you a turn," I said. "I want you to turn as far as you can on the backswing, feeling your left shoulder go under your chin, letting your left heel come up, loading your weight onto your right leg. I want your back facing the target at the finish of your backswing. Coming down, I want your left heel planted on the ground first thing to make for a full weight transfer, and I want you to swing all the way to a high finish facing your target. Don't worry where the ball goes. Just turn and turn and swing. Turn and turn. Turn and turn and swing."

In our first session, we started with a shag boy at the right edge of the tenth fairway. Because of the big turn, for the first time in his life John started hitting a wild hook. By the time we were halfway through the first bucket of balls, he had moved the shag boy all the way across the fairway, across the road and into a cornfield.

"Don't worry about the hook," I said. "We are adding yards now. When the time comes, we'll cure the hook. Just remember that what you will be learning over the next few months will enable you to play better golf for your entire life."

John had been playing with a restricted lower body. I taught him to use his lower body in the turn, with his shoulders, arms and hips all turning in one piece. It was a rotational movement, much like Paul Runyan's famous "turn in a barrel" advice but a little less precise, with more abandon.

He was wild, but he still wasn't long. As days and weeks went by, I saw John getting frustrated. I used to do what I called "pass by's" on the practice range, and when I would come to John I would always stop and encourage him.

"John, the great players like Sam Snead can always reach back and get an extra twenty yards when they want," I said. "They do it by making a bigger turn. You just stay at it. You're getting there."

It was a couple of months before John started hitting the ball solidly on the clubface every so often. It would go so far when he hit it flush that the sight and feeling kept up his spirits.

Some of my players went to watch the Texas Open in San Antonio one year while John was in school. Mike Souchak was the hottest player on tour at the moment, bashing his drives out of sight.

"John, I don't want you watching Mike Souchak," I said. "When you get to San Antonio, you go find Dale Douglas and watch him. Dale is about your build. You want to copy his swing, not Souchak's."

John and I began our distance project in September. Christmas came and went. He was longer, but not yet long enough and he was still wild.

Gradually more often John began hitting the ball on the screws. He was learning to trust himself. He would make that big turn back and big turn all the way through, and the more he believed it would produce a solid drive, the more it did.

Finally, after six months, our team was scheduled to play Texas A&M in a spring match. I scheduled John to play the Aggies' long hitting All-American Bobby Nichols.

Nichols beat John that day, but not off the tee. Every time Nichols blasted a tee ball, he would find John Trimble right there beside him.

John had gained fifty yards.

It was no short-term gain. Because of his dedication for six months, he had gained fifty yards for a lifetime of golf.

The last lesson I gave John was about forty years later when he was having trouble with his wedge. I told him he needed to make his club one inch longer, because tall men are inclined to bend over too much, but I never heard whether he did it. I hope he did, because the wedge is the third-most-important club in the bag, behind the putter and the driver.

Meanwhile John had married Frances, who is the director of the Texas Golf Hall of Fame, and they had a daughter, Tina, whom I started teaching golf when she was eleven years old. Tina was one of my best pupils. She's a teaching pro now.

With some of my pupils, like Kathy Whitworth, I never mentioned the turn because there was no need. With others, like John Trimble, getting that left shoulder back beneath the chin was something that had to be learned with tremendous effort. But if you ask John today, he'll tell you the effort has been repaid with many years of pleasure.

Practice It First

DURING A LABOR Day tournament at Austin Country Club, one of my college boys, Davis Love, Jr., hit his approach shot into a bunker on the first hole.

The ball was buried. Davis looked at it from all angles, but there was no way around it. He had to hit the ball out of the sand. It's the rules.

Davis blew it over the green and made a bogey.

On the second tee, I walked over to Davis and asked, "Do you practice that buried-lie shot very much?"

"No, Coach, I never practice it," he said.

"Davis, for the rest of this tournament I want you to stop hitting your approach shots into bunkers," I said. "You're liable to get another buried lie, and I don't want you to hit that shot again until you have practiced it."

Later that afternoon, I saw Davis in a practice bunker hitting ball after ball from buried lies. He became an expert at that shot. But not without practicing it now and then.

Take It to the Course

I HEARD ABOUT a high school player in Tyler named Marshall Pengra. I knew several schools were offering him scholarships, so I wrote him a letter that said, "We can't offer anything fancy, but we'll feed you and give you a place to sleep, and you'll be playing for a winning team if you come to Texas."

Marshall and his father drove to Austin to see me. I handed Marshall a 5-iron, just to see how he held the club. I asked him to hit a couple of balls. He was nervous and didn't hit his best shots, but I could tell from his grip and his stance that he would make a good player.

I played a round of golf with Marshall and his father, and afterward they agreed that the University of Texas was where Marshall would get his education.

In his freshman year I noticed that Marshall was usually on the practice range and not very often on the golf course.

One afternoon I asked why he was involved with such heavy practice.

"Coach, I'm trying to build a repeating swing," he said.

I said, "That's a noble thought, but the practice tee can become a big problem, you know."

"Why is that?" he asked

"Because if you are doing something that keeps your swing from repeating, it may be a very subtle thing, and the more you practice it, the more you ingrain it into your swing without knowing it. I want you to take your game onto the golf course. If you have a problem on the golf course, we'll take a look at that problem later on the practice tee."

"Do you think I'm ready to qualify for the team?" he asked.

"You have a good grip, good hands and good balance," I said. "You're already a lot more ready than most people in the world."

A good grip, good balance and a good attitude make you a winner.

The Gold Dust Twin

I WENT TO see the Legends of Golf one morning during the last year before that immensely important tournament, which began in Austin, was moved out of the Barton Creek Club and on to another time zone in the West.

I had been at the first Legends many years earlier at Onion Creek, a good club course a few minutes' drive south of downtown. The Legends was born at Onion

Creek and became the Senior Tour. At that first Legends, we didn't know if there would be a second.

Jimmy Demaret had a lot to do with the PGA declaring a player a senior at age fifty. Amateurs in the USGA do not become seniors until age fifty-five. Demaret wanted to be sure Arnold Palmer would be joining the seniors as soon as possible.

I wish the Legends had stayed at Onion Creek. It's a beautiful place to walk, with big oak and pecan trees and the creek winding through. Onion Creek and the Legends made history. They had an extra hole playoff with several of the biggest names in golf—Tommy Bolt and Roberto DeVicenzo, among others—firing at the pins and making an astonishing string of birdies on national television. I think that was very important in the development of the Senior Tour. The Legends let Mickey Wright and Kathy Whitworth play as a team one year. The women did so well they were never invited back.

At my last visit to the Legends, I wanted to see Harold McSpaden. Harold was, I believe, eighty-four and competing in the tournament.

Back when Byron Nelson had his year of winning eleven tournaments in a row, Harold finished second thirteen times and also won a few. That record on today's tour would earn him millions.

The newspapers called Harold by the nickname of Jug, and they called Harold and Byron together the Gold Dust Twins because they seemed to win everything.

At eighty-four Harold's swing was less than shoulder high, but he still had a fast hip turn and he hit his tee ball well over two hundred yards.

Visiting Harold again gave me great pleasure, and I loved what he did in the tournament. There was a special prize of twenty-five thousand dollars for the player who shot better than his age the most.

Harold turned in a 74 and 75. He was 19 under par for age.

For this he picked up the biggest check of any single tournament in his entire illustrious career as a Gold Dust Twin.

Harold designed a famous course called Dub's Dread in Piper, Kansas. Dub's Dread was 8,100 yards long in the beginning, with a par of 78. But over the years the course has been "shortened" to 7,800 yards—with four par 3s of more than 220 yards—and a par of 72.

Who holds the record at Dub's Dread? Jug McSpaden, the Gold Dust Twin, with a 68.

Treat the Easy Ones with Respect

I WAS SITTING in my cart under the oak trees at our course beside the river, watching a woman touring pro who was practicing on our putting green. She didn't know I was watching. I was supposed to give her a putting lesson, but sometimes I like to hide and observe for a while first.

As I was peeking from behind the trees, she missed ten consecutive three-foot putts. Every putt was missed one or two inches to the right of the hole. I had never seen anything like it.

"Are you doing that on purpose?" I called to her.

She looked around and saw me driving toward her out of the trees.

"Did you see me miss those putts?" she said.

"I could hardly believe my eyes."

"I just couldn't get lined up," she said.

I stopped my cart in the thick grass beside the green.

I said I hadn't ever noticed that she stepped back and looked at the line from behind the ball before any of her missed putts.

"It's only a three-footer," she said. "This isn't the Open."

"It still counts a stroke both here and at the Open," I said. "Promise me you will always step back and approach every putt from behind for the rest of your life, whether it's practice or the real thing."

"Okay," she said.

"Now, let's repeat this procedure with ten consecutive three-foot putts."

I squared up her stance and made sure her eyes were straight above the ball, and told her the backward and forward stroke should be the same length.

"But the main point is, never take a short putt for granted. Always approach the ball from behind, and make a practice stroke or two, and hit your putt on the sweet spot," I said.

Doing it this way she sank ten in a row.

"Watch me hit some longer putts," she said.

I said, "No, that's enough to think about for one lesson. Treat every putt with respect. Always stick with your entire putting plan for each putt. Always take care with each and every putt, no matter how easy it looks. Call this a lesson that will save you many strokes over a lifetime."

Scholarships

UNTIL THE MID-1950s, the USGA had a rule of amateur status that said if you had a college scholarship to play golf, other than the Chick Evans fund scholarships, you were not an amateur.

The NCAA did not have a parallel rule. Technically you could have a golf scholarship, according to the NCAA, but if you did and the USGA knew about it, you were forbidden from playing in any USGA events, such as the National Amateur and the Walker Cup.

This accounts for why Miller Barber had a football scholarship at Arkansas, and Bobby Nichols attended Texas A&M as a football player, and some other college stars of the period were carried on basketball and track squads.

We didn't hide our players at Texas, and we paid them handsomely. Each boy got a brand new sleeve of balls before every match.

Bibb's Cure for Lungers

MY OLD FRIEND Bibb Falk took Shoeless Joe Jackson's place in left field for the Chicago White Sox in 1920, the year after the Black Sox Scandal at the World Series caused Jackson to be thrown out of the game for life.

After a long and successful pro baseball career, Bibb came to the University of Texas as baseball coach in 1940. Two years later he went away to war, but he returned to coach at Texas for another twenty-odd years, making twenty-five in all.

One reason I mention the number of years Bibb coached is that I was golf coach at Texas for thirty-three years, ending in 1963.

Bibb's teams and my teams each won twenty Southwest Conference championships. Bibb won two national championships, and as coach I had one national intercollegiate champion, Ed White.

Bibb loved golf. He was one of the wildest hitters off the tee I ever played with regularly. Bibb got a thrill out of hitting home runs, to left, center or right.

I went to see his teams play at the old Clark Field, our wonderful little ballpark on the campus that had a hill running up the fence in center field.

One afternoon I dropped by to watch Bibb put his team through a practice. I always thought observing great coaches was a path toward becoming one.

There was a tall, skinny outfielder at the plate taking batting practice. The boy had a good eye and could make contact with the ball, but he lunged forward when he hit it and thus lost his power.

This is such a common problem in golf that I was curious how Bibb would deal with it in his own sport.

I have written about Leaping Lucifer, the worst lunger I ever saw. This boy at Texas was not in that category, but he was persistent in his lunging. Bibb decided he had seen enough.

Bibb sent one of his student assistants off to find a length of clothesline where they hung the uniforms to dry. He instructed the batter to tie one end of the rope around his waist.

Bibb wrapped the other end of the line around both of his powerful hands and stood about twenty feet behind the hitter.

"Throw him one down the middle!" Bibb yelled.

The pitcher threw the ball, the outfielder swung his bat and tried to lunge forward—but Bibb dug in his heels and yanked the boy backward, sort of like a rodeo cowboy roping a calf.

"Throw him another!" Bibb yelled.

Again the pitcher threw, and this time the batter hit the ball solidly over second base, lunging a little less than before.

"You getting the idea? You stay home and hit the ball," Bibb said.

"Yes sir, I'm getting the idea," the boy replied.

Bibb stayed there for half an hour holding on to the clothesline tied around the boy's waist, as a couple of different pitchers stepped up to throw batting practice.

The boy learned. By the time Bibb ordered him untied, the boy was keeping his weight centered over the plate when he hit the ball instead of chasing out in front and losing his distance.

The boy said, with a big grin, "Coach, it's so much sweeter when I don't lunge."

For all these years since that time, I have remembered how Bibb cured the lunger. I have seen thousands of golfers who would have been helped greatly, I believe, by Bibb's method with the baseball player.

No, I have never done it. I have held the butt of a club against a player's head to keep it steady during the swing. I have stuck a shaft in the ground next to the pupil's left leg to show that the lunge would knock it over.

But I have never tied clothesline around a lunger's waist and ridden the pupil like livestock to haul back the forward leap.

For one thing, I weighed about 135 pounds in my prime, and I've seen golf lungers who could jerk me off my feet and drag me through the grass.

But the main reason I never did it is that it just doesn't seem like a proper thing to do.

I suppose the golf magazines will someday carry advertisements featuring the new miracle invention, a rope you can slip around your waist and wrap the other end around a telephone pole and cure your lunge. It was Bibb's idea.

You're on Your Own

HARRIS GREENWOOD PLAYED on my golf team in college, played in the U.S. Amateur, and then quit the game for about twenty-five years.

When he got the urge to take golf up again, Harris came to see me at our new course by the river.

"It's been so long since I've had a club in my hands that I can't remember how I used to swing," he said.

"Who would you want to swing like?"

I thought Harris would say Sam Snead. When he was in college, Harris's swing came over the top just a tad, as Snead's does.

"I want to swing like Ben Hogan," Harris said.

I looked at him and shook my head.

"Harris," I said, "I can't help you. Ben had to figure out his swing on his own, and if you want to swing like Ben, you'll need to resolve it for yourself."

Certainly I do not denigrate the swing of one of the top golfers in history. Ben's swing in his prime was awesome to watch.

I played with Ben when he was a young man with a big hook. I watched him change from a hooker to a fade, from a tough little competitor to a legend of the game. Ben did figure out his championship swing on his own, to fit his particular physique and personality and enhance his own virtues while blocking out his flaws.

I couldn't teach Ben's swing to anyone. Millions have

tried to copy it. A few, like Gardner Dickinson and George Knudson, came very close.

I would never try to teach a pupil to copy the swing of a genius. I always tried to give my pupils knowledge of the swing through mental pictures and muscular sensations, and we would hope for the pupil's own individual genius to emerge.

His Money's Worth

———

YEARS AGO WHEN Sam Snead used to give golf lessons, he was hitting practice balls at White Sulphur Springs, preparing for a tournament. A well-dressed, wealthy-looking fellow approached Sam and asked for a lesson.

Snead's first inclination was to tell the fellow to go away. But then Sam cast an eye at the expensive wardrobe on his prospective pupil. "Go get your clubs," Sam said.

Soon the fellow came trotting back to the practice range, put down his golf bag and pulled out his driver.

"Stick that driver back in your sack," Sam told him. "Today we are starting with your 9-iron. After we see how well you can handle your 9-iron, we'll start up the list and finally we'll reach your driver last."

The pupil scratched his chin and looked at Snead.

"How many lessons will this take?" the pupil asked.

"I don't know," said Sam.

"How much do you charge for a lesson?" the pupil asked.

Sam said his lessons were twenty-five dollars each.

"But I only want two dollars' worth," the pupil said.

"Then your time is up," said Sam. "You've already just had two dollars' worth."

Hit the Can

SUPPOSE YOU ARE strolling along the road with a walking stick in your hand. You see an old tin can in the road. You decide on impulse to give the can a hearty two-handed whack that will knock it into the grass.

How do you do it? Do you tense up and worry about keeping your head still? Of course you don't, but your fundamentals are always sound when you whack a tin can.

That's the freewheeling feeling you should have when you hit a golf ball.

More Distance

AT THE MENTION of the words "more distance," most golfers go on point like bird dogs, ears perked up, every sense aroused and curious.

More distance is the grail that nearly every average golfer seeks, despite the fact that everyone knows practice on the short game is the fastest and most certain way to lower scores.

Every teacher has many pupils who are bursting with desire to hit the ball farther off the tee. These pupils may keep losing skins to the good putters, but nevertheless they would rather hit soaring drives than learn to chip close to the hole.

Fundamental motions and thoughts that will produce more distance can be taught to almost anyone with some degree of success.

But I think the tremendously long hitters are born with the knack.

Ask long hitters where they get their power, and their answers differ on the sources but indicate that they pretty much had the distance all along.

Tommy Armour has been a major influence on my teaching. We disagree on only one important thing. Tommy insisted his pupils hold their heads rock still while they swing. At teaching seminars, he would say, "Hold that head still, hold it still!" I believe the head can move backward a bit, but never forward nor up nor down.

Tommy considered the steady head—and a good bash with the right hand—as the ingredients for his power.

But Tommy Armour could tear a deck of cards in half with his bare hands. The secret of his power, I believe, was his awesome natural strength combined with his gift of coordination.

Sam Snead was a tremendously long driver. He said his power came from his legs. Another long hitter, Henry Cotton, said his power came from his hands. Julius Boros is not usually mentioned among the long hitters, but he could put it out there with nearly anyone if he wanted. Julius said his power was the result of his shoulder turn. Lawson Little, one of the longest hitters of his day, believed his own power came from his back muscles.

One of the longest hitters in history, Jimmy Thomson, enjoyed coming to me for lessons because I encourage my pupils to hit the ball hard. Some other teachers wanted Jimmy to cut back on his power for the sake of more accuracy, but Jimmy would rather hit a wedge out of the rough than a 6-iron from the fairway. I loved watching Jimmy smash those drives.

A normal drive for Jimmy was about 300 yards. If he had tried to ease up and cut his drives back to 250, he would have been faced with the most difficult shot in golf—a let-up driver. Drivers are meant to be swung hard, and swinging hard was where Jimmy got his power.

When I told Jimmy to go ahead and hit it hard, that made me a wise teacher in his eyes.

I start my young pupils hitting the ball hard. I believe if you are taught early to baby the ball, you may never learn to drive for distance. You may develop a good-looking swing that is lacking in snap.

I don't mean swing from the heels on every drive. You must swing on balance. Like Boros, Jimmy Demaret was not noted as a long hitter, but he could reach back for something extra and belt it out there with Ben Hogan if he needed to.

When I wanted more distance as a player, I did it with a faster hip turn and a fast rotation of my whole left arm counterclockwise in the downswing, much the way Hogan did it.

But that is not the answer for everyone. A fast hip turn is dangerous for the average player, whose arms won't catch up with his body.

A retired general, Bob Hullender, who has played in

my tournament at Austin Country Club, is one of the longest hitting of the senior amateurs and winner of many prestigious tournaments.

General Hullender has two stainless-steel hips.

He started playing golf in his forties and was a low handicapper within two years. Because of osteoarthritis, Bob had one hip replaced. He built himself up with stretching and flexibility and other exercises. No sooner was he back on the golf course than his other hip began to hurt. Within a year, he had a second stainless-steel hip.

Billy Penn, a friend of the General, tells me Hullender hits five buckets of balls and also plays golf nearly every day.

"He only plays on days that end in 'y,' " Billy said.

The General has won several long driving contests with blows of more than three hundred yards.

How can he do this on two artificial hips?

Hullender has strong, limber hands and arms and makes a full turn with his powerful shoulders.

But I think the secret of his great distance is that before he took up golf, the General was a world-class softball fast-pitcher. He could fire that upshoot at the plate a hundred miles an hour.

This fast-pitch softball action will whip a clubhead through the ball in a blur.

Every time I start talking about distance, I return to my theme that the short game is what you should practice the most. Long driver that he is, General Hullender spends at least half of his practice time chipping and putting.

Distance alone is a thrill, but distance alone will never win you a tournament. As General Hullender knows, the short game wins tournaments.

Yet average golfers will always continue to pursue the

grail of more distance. It's in the nature of the game, I think, to seek the euphoria of sending your ball flying far through the sky and watching it drop to earth way down yonder.

Saving the Cow

AUSTIN HAS GROWN large now, and 45th Street is in the central part of town. In my early years as head pro, 45th Street was the north boundary of Austin. Our country club, the second oldest west of the Mississippi, was several hundred yards south of 45th Street. We were out in the country. It was beautiful out there, with pure, flowing creeks and giant oak trees, and fields of wildflowers in the spring.

A German family had a farm down the road from the club. A blue northern hit us early one September, which is ordinarily a good golfing month in Texas. The creeks became solid hunks of ice. Oak tree limbs cracked and broke under the weight of ice. We stoked up the stove in the golf shop and our regulars huddled around it.

A member came in and said the German family was having a problem with one of the cows at their farm. Because of the slippery ice, they couldn't get the cow into their barn. The German farmers had studied the situation. They had decided to wrap a thick blanket of hay around the cow and cover her with a tarp.

For the next week our members sat around the fire

and waited for the weather to break and pondered what should be done about the cow. The owners were bringing food and water every day, but still the ground was too slippery for the cow's hooves to traverse the ice all the way to the barn.

Over the history of our club, most of the great men of Texas have passed through. We've had the most powerful politicians, the richest tycoons, the brainiest professors and Supreme Court Justices among our membership or as guests.

While the ice storm lasted, I cleaned and polished clubheads and shaved a number of hickory shafts. I would step into the front of the shop and hear my members discussing that stranded cow as they watched the long icicles draping the trees.

Many plans were hatched to deal with that cow. Straps and trusses and teams of mules were suggested. Finally it was decided that the wisest course was to let the cow stay where she was until the ice melted.

After six or seven days, one of our members struggled through the ice into the golf shop with the news that the cow was safe in the German family's barn.

"How'd they do it?" the hot stove crowd wanted to know.

"I hear one of our caddies showed up and tied gunnysacks over the cow's hooves and just walked her home."

Jimmy Would Have Changed His Grip

DURING OUR MANY years as friends and colleagues, Jimmy Demaret and I had countless conversations about the golf grip. You may be surprised to discover that when Jimmy was Masters champion and known the world over for his ability, he decided his grip was wrong—but he was too far into a successful career to think seriously about changing it.

Jimmy used the familiar Vardon, or overlapping, grip from his early days as a caddie all the way to the end of his life. Yet he came to believe the Vardon grip is not the most fundamentally sound grip for most players, including Jimmy himself.

Harry Vardon made the piggybacking of the pinkie finger of his right hand onto the top of his left index finger—or into the space between the index and third fingers—into the most popular way for players to hold the club.

Vardon had big, strong, fast hands, and his style of grip was meant to move his hands closer together and, by removing one finger from the handle, reduce the possibility of his right hand overpowering his left during his swing. Proper application of his hands increased his power and helped him to control the club.

"But how many golfers do we encounter whose big problem is having too much power?" Jimmy would say.

Jimmy believed the average player should learn the so-called ten-finger grip. In fact, it is eight fingers and two thumbs, but you know what I mean.

This is often called the baseball grip, which is incorrect. If you were to grip a golf club like a baseball bat, your thumbs would be around the handle just as your fingers are.

"The full-fingered grip is the most fundamentally sound grip for the vast majority of golfers," Jimmy said. "Most golfers don't need to fight hands that are too fast. Most golfers have just the opposite problem—their hands are not fast enough."

In the full-fingered grip, Jimmy believed, the hands should be as close together as possible, with that right pinkie finger on the handle of the club to help deliver the blow.

"In a reasonable swing, the right hand won't take over from the left with the full-fingered grip," Jimmy said. "The two hands will work together. You get more power and better control. I'm so accustomed to the Vardon grip by now that it would take me a long time to change, and I'm doing okay the way things are. But if I was a newcomer to the game, or an average player who doesn't depend on golf for a living, I would certainly use the full-fingered grip."

Some top players use the full-fingered grip. Johnny Revolta, Bob Rosburg, Art Wall, Beth Daniel, and Alice Ritzman come to mind. Johnny said he felt the full-fingered grip helped him stay behind and inside the ball and also made his release through the shot free and full. Alice was at a disadvantage when she first went on the tour because of her lack of length off the tee. I asked her to try the full-fingered grip. She did and her distance picked up considerably.

Looking back on my teaching career, I believe now

that I should have taught the full-fingered grip to nearly every woman pupil, with the exception of powerful hitters like Babe Zaharias and Mickey Wright.

Perhaps I should have taught it to more men, as well. The full-fingered grip, with the hands properly placed, can be just as pretty to my eye as the Vardon grip.

There is no doubt that putting that one extra finger on the handle will supply a bit more authority when your clubhead whips through the ball.

Like Jimmy, I grew up as a caddie using the Vardon grip because it was the most popular grip among the players I watched and copied. I love the Vardon grip. I have taught it with great care for a very long time.

But if you are having trouble putting a solid smack on the ball, give the full-fingered grip a try. Watch that you hold your club lightly, especially with the right. Put your right thumb on the left side of the handle, where it can't jump in and take over your swing.

Thinking about Jimmy, I recall that he took golf lessons from only one man in his entire life. That man was the revered teacher Jack Burke, Sr., at River Oaks in Houston.

As a youngster, Jimmy went to work for Jack as an assistant in the golf shop. Jack told Jimmy one of the benefits of the job was that Jimmy could play golf at River Oaks all he wanted.

"Just so long as you do it before six in the morning," Jack said.

The First Team

—

ONE OF THE major events in golf in my part of the world for a long time has been the Texas Cup Matches. A team of professionals plays against a team of amateurs for bragging rights and a nice trophy.

The matches began in 1933 at Brook Hollow in Dallas. The first pro team was Francis Scheider, Howard Estep, Larry Nabholtz, George Aulbach, Willie Maguire, Ben Hogan, Byron Nelson, Jack Grout, Francis McGonagill, Levi Lynch, Graham Ross and yours truly.

We pros won, but not without a struggle. Most of the crowd followed the match between Scheider, the Brook Hollow pro who gave Betty Jameson her first lessons, and the world-class amateur Gus Moreland. Gus had beaten Byron earlier in the finals of the Glen Garden Invitation in Fort Worth.

Francis won the match 1-up.

Everybody knows that Ben Hogan and Byron Nelson went on to become champions of the world outside Texas, but many may not be aware that Jack Grout went on to Scioto Country Club in Columbus, Ohio, where he became the first and primary teacher of a young fellow named Jack Nicklaus.

Jimmie Connolly

WHEN I FIRST saw Jimmie Connolly, he was a scrappy little caddie at our first country club in Hancock Park. A boy didn't just show up and become a caddie. You had to be accepted by the other boys, as well as by the caddie master. If my big brother, Tom, a powerful fellow, had not been the king of the caddie yard when I was a boy, my life might have taken an entirely different path.

Jimmie was the favorite caddie of Bob Connerly, who was always called Mr. Bob. Mr. Bob played crosshanded, used five clubs and won the state championship four or five times. He would hardly ever enter our clubhouse. Mr. Bob didn't keep a locker. A stranger who saw him out there swinging crosshanded and using a little canvas bag with few clubs would have bet the family fortune he could beat Mr. Bob, but that stranger would have left the course broke.

As a young head pro, I hired Jimmie as my caddie master. I knew if there was any problem in the yard, Jimmie would handle it. On Shoal Creek near the club there were a bunch of boys called "the Creekers." They were known as a hearty lot, and many of them became our caddies. Jimmie and I were remembering "the Creekers" recently. Every one of them who went through our caddie yard education turned out to be a fine citizen.

In those days, there was no such thing as a forty-hour work week for most people. Offices stayed open until noon on Saturdays. Knowing my businessmen and doctors wouldn't arrive at the club until lunch, I let my caddies play the course on Saturday mornings, so long as they were back in the caddie yard before noon. This is how Jimmie learned to play.

Before long, Jimmie worked his way up to being my shop assistant. He was never a registered professional, but he could repair a golf club as well as any pro.

Jimmie had a very strong grip in his early career as a player. He hooked every shot. I told him, "Jimmie, one of these days those hooks are going to quit coming back into the fairway. We better fix that grip."

It took a month of steady practice for Jimmie to get his grip right, and after that he became a wonderful golfer. He won our city championship and the Texas state championship. He asked if I thought he should try playing with the pros. I told him, "Jimmie, you have made such good friends through golf, I think you might be happier if you went into business. I know you'd have a world of customers."

When Jimmie quit working for me to go into the insurance business, the members of Austin Country Club voted to give him a lifetime honorary membership. That doesn't happen often at any country club, but our members didn't want to lose a player of Jimmie's quality. Besides, everybody liked Jimmie and wanted to see him often. He stayed with us and won our club championship several times.

I hired Jimmie's brother Willard to replace him in the shop and got chewed out for it by my brother, Tom. Willard had been working in Tom's shop at Austin Muny and was a valued employee.

Many years later, Jimmie became one of the people responsible for beginning the tournament called the Legends of Golf, which was the start of the Senior Tour.

Senior Tour players making big money these days ought to tip their caps to Jimmie Connolly.

Jimmie was a close friend of Jimmy Demaret. One year Jimmie and Charlie Crenshaw, Ben's father, were playing as a team in the Champions cup matches in Houston. With another friend, Rex Kitchens, they told Jimmie about a thousand acres of land they knew of in south Austin along Onion Creek.

"It's a perfect site for a golf course," Jimmie told him.

Demaret drove to Austin and walked the land with them. He agreed that this land should hold a beautiful golf course. Jimmie and Charlie brought in their brothers as partners, and more investors, including the big timberman Arthur Temple, joined them, and after a number of obstacles were overcome, Jimmy Demaret began designing a golf course for the first time.

One obstacle was a steady supply of water. Onion Creek may be several hundred yards wide at flood, but you can step over it during a drought. A golf course must have constant water. The nearest aquifer they could tap was two miles west. Mr. Kitchens owned all but one plot of land between the club and the water. The man who owned the land refused to speak to them, and had his son phone and tell them to leave him alone.

Jimmie Connolly and Charlie Crenshaw went to the fellow's house to reason with him. They saw him sitting on the porch, his chair tilted back against the wall, chin on his chest, hat tilted over his eyes.

"We might as well go home," Charlie said.

But Jimmie walked up to the front step and said, "Sir, I wonder if we could have a moment of your time for something that is very important to us?"

The man seemed to nod.

"Just east of here, we own some property, and—"

Jimmie went no further. The man stood up and

153

shouted, "You get away from me, and don't you ever come back!"

The pipeline they dug from the aquifer to Onion Creek went around the forbidden land, about a mile longer than if they could have dug it in a straight line.

While they were solving the water problem, Jimmie told me Demaret would lay out the bunkers with a length of rope, and then they would paint in the outline and start digging.

Demaret built a course that is great fun to play for those of all skills. The expert will run into problems the average player may never notice. The first nine is easy to walk and quite attractive to the eye. There are many trees, and Onion Creek flows through the course.

When Fred Raphael came up with the idea for the first Legends of Golf tournament, he phoned Jimmy Demaret in Houston to ask for his support.

"Great idea. I'm all for it," Demaret said.

"Which of your two courses at Champions do you want to hold it on?" Raphael asked, meaning the two eighteen-hole courses at the Champions Club that Jimmy and Jack Burke, Jr., built in Houston.

"I've got the perfect place for a tournament like this," Jimmy said. "It's in Austin. It's called Onion Creek."

I like to think that one of our Austin Country Club caddie yard graduates, Jimmie Connolly, not only was a great player in his own right, but made an important contribution to the health and future of the game.

Look Again

ON THE FOURTEENTH green at the Masters one year, Jackie Burke, Jr., had a twenty-foot putt that needed to roll over a hump on its way to the hole.

Jackie studied the putt. His caddie studied the putt. Finally his caddie straightened up and said, "It breaks about a foot."

"Which way?" Jackie asked.

"Well, now I have to look again," said his caddie.

Hazards

MANY AVERAGE AND high-handicap players get nervous at the sight of a hazard and try to aim well away from it.

What often happens is that the hazard is at the top of their thoughts, and as they swing their bodies overcompensate for their aim, and the path of the club knocks the ball straight into the hazard they were concentrating on avoiding. This happens more often than you may think.

Sometimes the opposite happens, and it is just as bad. The player aims away from a hazard on the left, let's say, and then hits a wild slice.

A friend was telling me recently about a game he played at Sawgrass Country Club in Ponte Vedra, Florida. The ninth hole at Sawgrass West has water running the length of it on the left. On the ninth tee, my friend told his partner, "No matter what you do, don't hit your drive into the water."

His partner took a mighty slash at the ball, and the next thing they heard was the sound of shattering glass.

His partner had sliced his drive clean off the course and broken a plate-glass window in the living room of a home.

Usually I tell my pupils to take notice of the hazard but then ignore it and go ahead and take dead aim at a spot on the fairway. With some pupils, I tell them to aim at the hazard if they're really scared of it, and see if their golfing minds will respond by hooking or slicing the ball away from the object of their dread.

Strike a Match

ONE TEACHING AID I used to use was a box of kitchen matches.

I would escort one of my college players out to the asphalt parking lot, open the box and scatter kitchen matches on the ground.

Then I would tell the college boy to take his 7-iron and strike fire from those match heads with his golf swing.

This was a sure cure for hitting behind the ball and also a great aid to concentrating on the point of your aim.

If your mind wandered, you could sprain your wrist or put a nasty mark on the bottom of your club.

I used the kitchen matches on Betty Jameson when she first came to me for lessons, and later I did it with Mickey Wright, also.

Betty and Mickey could make that asphalt parking lot look like the Fourth of July.

The two of them hit the ball exactly at the bottom of their swings more precisely than any golfers I have ever seen. They could really strike those matches.

Not Quite Gentlemen

DURING MY YOUTH as a caddie, golf professionals were not allowed to enter the clubhouse through the front door, or to be seen in the dining room. Golf professionals were regarded as curious persons but not as gentlemen fit to mingle with proper society.

Walter Hagen arrived on the scene with his powerful charm and his champion's game, and things began to change around him.

Inverness was the first club to invite professionals into the clubhouse. I heard about it as a sixteen-year-old caddie.

After the U.S. Open in 1920, Hagen and a few other

professionals presented the Inverness Club with a tall, chiming clock, set into a handsome wood stand with a poem on a brass plate.

The poem says:

> God measures men by what they are,
> Not in what wealth possess.
> This vibrant message chimes afar
> The voice of Inverness.

Salute from a Friend

IT WAS A shock to all of us when Jimmy Demaret passed away suddenly. Jimmy had friends all over the world. Not only was he a champion golfer, he was a singer, a comedian, a good companion and a person with a big heart.

I have a copy of a letter written by Ben Hogan as a salute to Jimmy, who was probably the best friend Ben ever had among his fellow golfers. Tears come to my eyes every time I read the letter, especially the last two paragraphs, which I quote:

"As partners, you and I never lost a four ball match, and, although I will be a little tardy in joining you, I want you to keep practicing so that one day we can win another four ball together.

"I send to you my admiration and thanks for all the nice things you have done for me and others—you helped make my bad times more bearable and my good times better. You were my friend and I miss you. May you sleep in peace and I will join you later."

Willie the Weeper

———

IN MY CADDIE days there was a boy in the yard named Willie. He was about twelve years old, wore bib overalls and lived in a cabin on Shoal Creek with his folks, who made a living chopping cedars and catching catfish.

Willie was a good caddie. He was known for never losing a ball. Off the first tee the carry was over a flower garden and a road in those days, and Willie always found his player's ball if it was topped or popped up. He was in steady demand and sometimes was tipped as much as fifteen cents, which before World War I was big money to a kid.

But Willie was never happy. As far as Willie was concerned, the weather was always too hot or too cold, too wet or too dry, too windy or too still. The bread that he brought from home had too much butter on it, or not enough.

He usually had a headache. His feet hurt. Nothing was just the way he wanted it to be. My big brother, Tom, was the boss among the caddies. Tom got fed up listening to Willie's complaints and probably would have run him off except that Willie was popular with members. Willie never opened his mouth around a member, but he seldom shut it in the caddie yard.

Some of the boys started calling him Willie the Weeper.

To hear Willie tell it, he never had any luck, either. The breaks always went against him. Providence had a grudge against Willie, in his point of view. Life was not fair.

One morning in the caddie yard under a mighty oak tree, Willie was swinging at small stones with an old hickory-shafted niblick a member had given him. One of the small stones turned out to be the tip of a large rock that was buried in the earth. The hickory shaft snapped in half.

"Look at that, will you?" Willie wailed. "Why does everything bad have to happen to me? It isn't fair!"

My brother, Tom, had a commanding presence, even as a boy. He walked over to Willie and said, "You want to change your life?"

"I want to get lucky, if that's what you mean."

"There's two things you've got to understand," Tom said. "The first is, nobody ever promised you life would be fair. The second is, to change your life you have to change the way you think."

Willie looked at the expression on Tom's face and decided not to complain about anything at that moment. A few days later Willie's folks packed up and moved farther out into the Hill Country, and I never saw him again. I heard he joined the Marine Corps and served in France.

I don't know if Willie took Tom's words to heart.

However, I do know that I never forgot them.

Too Far Forward

IN MY OPINION, most golfers play the ball too far forward in their stance.

This is one of the main reasons for average golfers to swing from the outside to the inside—they are trying to catch up to the ball position. I've heard many professionals comment that their ball position keeps creeping forward, and they have to stop and make themselves play it farther back.

Ralph and Howard

IN THE MIDDLE of the 1930s, when I was president of the Texas PGA, the best golfer in the world was a quiet, good-looking fellow named Ralph Guldahl, who grew up in Dallas and played out of the Cedar Crest Club.

Ralph won the U.S. Open twice in a row and won three Western Opens, then considered a major, winning all five prestigious titles in a period of three years. Earlier he had been beaten by one shot for the U.S. Open in 1933 by Johnny Goodman, the last amateur to win that championship.

I watched Ralph on the practice range in many sessions. His swing was compact and simple, and he hit the ball straight. What needed help was his putting, which soon became quite good.

For some reason, the crowds and the reporters were not drawn to Ralph, even though he was a tall, handsome man. He was a conservative dresser and a quiet person, like I am. Jimmy Demaret used to say, "Harvey, make a noise, so we'll know you haven't left." Ralph didn't have any buddies. I was probably as close to him as anyone in golf at that time.

Years after Ralph more or less gave up tournament golf to take a head pro job in St. Louis, he told me a story about one of his trips to Los Angeles, where Ralph played a lot of golf at Bel Air with a wealthy, show business crowd.

Ralph told me he had met Howard Hughes, who was a billionaire back when there weren't many of them. Hughes played at Bel Air. He carried a low handicap, a 2, I believe Ralph said.

Hughes asked Ralph to watch him hit some iron shots. Ralph was happy to do so. Ralph straightened Hughes's posture a little and moved the ball back a little in his stance, nothing more.

"How much do I owe you?" Hughes asked when Ralph was ready to leave.

"Why, nothing, it was my pleasure," Ralph said.

"You're a pro, Ralph," said Hughes.

Ralph went off to meet his wife and watch one of their horses run at Hollywood Park.

The next morning a bellhop brought an envelope to the door of the Guldahls' suite.

Ralph opened the envelope. He read a note that said, "Thanks for the lesson." Then he looked at the check inside. Hughes had sent him $15,000.

Ralph wondered if he should accept the money, because he had only been trying to be friendly, and giving golf tips was just a way to be social.

He decided that Hughes was trying to be friendly, and writing checks was just his own way of being social, so Ralph took his wife shopping.

Harvey Penick
Award Dinner, 1994
Honoring
Rep. J. J. Jake Pickle

Invocation

Give me a few good lies, Oh Lord
and the poise to make my life shots work.
Give me healthy mind, Oh Lord
to keep the good and pure in sight,
which seeing sin is not struck dumb,
but finds a way to set it right.
Give me a mind that is not bored
that does not whimper, whine, or sigh.
Don't let me worry overmuch about that
fussy thing called I.

Give me a sense of humor Lord.
Permit me the grace to see a joke,
to find some happiness in life and
pass it on to other folk.

—Monsignor Richard C. McCabe

A Mystery Is Solved

FOR MANY YEARS Jimmie Connolly would arrive at the club near Riverside Drive regularly at high noon. He would park his car, new each season, behind the clubhouse. He would leave his keys in the car—a common thing in those days in Austin, when most people we knew never bothered to lock their houses. Jimmie would head straight for the first tee. After a round of golf and a bit of socializing in the grill, Jimmie would go out to his car and drive home for dinner. It seemed Jimmie kept getting a lemon each time he traded for a newer car. His cars never got the gas mileage that other fellows claimed to get.

One day Jimmie was out on the course and remembered something he had left in his car, a pair of glasses, maybe. Jimmie walked back to the clubhouse, went around to the parking lot—and his car was gone.

We didn't call the police. Instead we sat and waited. Sure enough, at 3:15 in the afternoon, a few minutes before Jimmie would ordinarily be finishing his round, his new car wheeled into the parking lot being driven by the friend of a caddie.

We quickly got to the bottom of the plot. While Jimmie had been predictably out on the golf course every day between noon and 3:30 P.M., a few of the boys had taken turns spinning around town in Jimmie's new car.

I think Jimmie was sort of relieved to find out. The gas mileage curse had been a burden on his mind.

Solid

MY SON, TINSLEY, brought me a book that breaks the golf swing down into fifty-some "simple steps."

I studied the book. I have no quarrel with anyone who loves to examine golf in a scientific way. If you need to break the swing down into fifty-some positions, this book does a good job of it.

My approach is different.

I try to teach a swing that is all one motion that cannot be broken down into positions or else it will cease being one motion. My ideal is to teach my pupil to hit the ball solidly with his or her own best personal swing.

Solid is what you want in golf.

Check Your Hips

———

HUNDREDS OF SEASONED players have come to me with suffering and confusion written on their faces and have voiced the plaintive complaint that usually begins, "I have forgotten how to play golf. After all these years, my swing has left me. I feel as if I have never picked up a golf club in my life."

These are usually middle handicappers, and often they are middle-aged, as well, but this malady can strike any golfer of any age, even the experts and the young.

The first thing I do is reassure them. "Your swing hasn't left you," I say. "Something has inserted itself between your golfing mind and your muscles, and we had best get busy and find out what it is."

In most cases I have already guessed what is the root of the problem, and how to cure it, but I always start at the beginning by taking a look at the pupil's grip and address. If the grip and address are all right, then I am pretty sure that the problem is caused by a golf tip that has been so overdone that it has caused the pupil to forget one of the basic aspects of the swing—the turning of the hips.

It happens all the time. A pupil will read in a book or a magazine, or perhaps see on a television instructional, that such and such a thing should be done—like, perhaps, taking the club straight back from the ball for the first few inches—and this tip will appear to work wonders instantly.

So the pupil will concentrate on this tip to the exclusion of nearly all else, and the first thing you know, the pupil's golf swing has become a total stranger.

As I always say, golf tips are like aspirin. One may do you good, but if you swallow the whole bottle you will be lucky to survive.

Some fashionable teachers today stress a big shoulder turn with the hip turn severely limited. This, they say, creates a windup, a powerful tension between the shoulders and the hips that, when unleashed, creates tremendous power.

This is true, but it also creates the lower back pain that afflicts so many golfers, expert and dub alike.

Take the word of Bobby Jones or Ben Hogan, whose swings look very different but who agree that the biggest difference in ball striking between the good player and the high handicapper is most often in the use of the hips.

Pupils frequently tell me, "But it says in all the books that the hips should turn forty-five degrees and the shoulders ninety degrees."

That is fine, but too many players make an effort to hold their hip turns to forty-five degrees and wind up with no hip turn at all.

If you feel that your swing has gone away to some mysterious place, that the smack of authority has vanished from your golf, I am going to say right now that it is probably because you are not turning your hips.

If you make a good, full hip turn, both backward and forward, your swing will come back and the authority will return along with it.

One way to make a good hip turn is to turn your belly button to the right until you can feel your weight on your right heel, and then turn your belly button to the left until it is pointing at your target and your weight is on your left foot.

Another way to start the hip turn is by turning your right hip pocket backward until it almost faces your target.

However you decide to do it, be sure you make a turning motion, a rotation of the hips, and not a rocking motion that transfers your weight from one foot to the other without actually turning at all. I see this much too often.

I like to tell my pupils to turn as if shaking hands with someone on each side. It's the "Howdy do?" move.

Just make sure your belly button goes along on the ride. In fact, your belly button should be the engine that drives the movement.

Always remember, if your golf swing is not performing but your grip and stance are all right, check your hips.

The Trouble with Money

ONE OF THE questions I have been asked most often is why I have always charged so little for lessons and in fact have often given them for nothing.

The simple answer is that I teach people, not a golf swing. I don't want to feel obligated to try to make a person change if I see he or she is unwilling to do so. I think it is the pupil's duty to learn to hit the ball at the bottom of the swing, and it is the teacher's duty to show the pupil how to make the clubface square when it contacts the ball.

Swinging my favorite training aid—the old-fashioned weed cutter—will instill in the pupil the feeling of hitting through the ball at the bottom of the swing. Picturing one of my favorite pieces of advice—clipping off the tee or brushing the grass—will give your muscles the feeling of hitting with a square clubface.

I have avoided contracting for a series of lessons because if I see that a pupil is unwilling to put his or her best attention to trying these simple things, then I will be wasting time for both of us.

I put myself in the pupil's shoes and ask myself: how would I feel if I paid a golf pro a lot of money for a lesson, and I look up after ten minutes and see the pro has gone away?

I could stay with even the most obstinate pupil for the full period and insist on him or her learning different positions for the club to be in during the swing, but this would just be a way of making the pupil think he or she is getting his or her money's worth. It would be teaching a swing, not a person.

I had rather be free to disappear in a few minutes if I'm not getting anywhere, or just as free to stay for hours if I am doing the pupil a lot of good, rather than money having anything to do with our relationship.

Reading the Mountain

ONE SPRING MY golf team drove to Colorado Springs in a University of Texas station wagon to play in a tournament at the Broadmoor.

My boys fared poorly in the tournament because they missed a lot of putts. They had a hard time reading the breaks in the greens. Many putts at Broadmoor look as if they are going one way when instead they are going the opposite direction. To putt those greens, you must take into account the slope of the mountain—a factor my boys kept forgetting.

"I'll tell you how poorly we read the place," said Sonny Rhodes, one of my top players who went on to become a fine teacher and club pro. "When it was time to come home, our station wagon wouldn't start. We all got out and pushed, but we couldn't make the station wagon go anywhere.

"Finally we stopped pushing and looked the situation over again. You know what? We looked at the slope of the mountain and realized we had been trying to push the station wagon uphill!"

Good Putters Have Faith

—————

It is a characteristic of good putters that if they miss a putt in the makeable range, they will nearly always blame spike marks or the grain or some fault in the green. The reason for this is that good putters have faith in their ability to make a good stroke every time.

One difference between good putters and mediocre putters is that a good putter's ball will catch the edge of the hole and drop in, whereas a mediocre putter's ball will catch the edge of the hole and spin out.

Another thing I believe about putting is that it is always better to hit your putt toward the toe of the club rather than toward the heel. A putt hit toward the heel will go up to the hole and slide to the left.

In Byron's Prime

—————

I was chatting with Byron Nelson about the difference in the way golf is played today and the way it was played in our prime, and we agreed that the main thing is the condition of the golf courses.

Byron said, "Today the turf on the fairways is nearly always in good shape, and a really bad lie is a rare thing. In earlier times, we played on fairways that now would be considered Ground Under Repair. There's more contour in the greens today than when I was young, but the greens now are smooth and uniform. It used to be that when we had a fifteen-foot putt, we had to hit it. I mean really hit it, because the grass was tall, if there was any grass, and the ground was bumpy. These days with a fifteen-footer, you just roll it."

A major change in the way golf is played came with the good fairway turf. It used to be necessary to hit down hard on those bare lies to get the ball up in the air. Now more shots can be swept away.

Byron and I also agreed that the reason Texas produced so many good players was that the wind seemed to be blowing always, and the condition of the courses forced players to learn to hit all kinds of shots. This was before courses were irrigated and manicured. Texas courses could be compared, at least in conditioning, to the famous old courses in Scotland. If it rained, the course was green. If it didn't rain, the course was brown.

The most important change in golf equipment, we decided, was in the shaft. Being lighter, the shaft can be swung faster and the ball goes farther.

I first met Byron at the Texas Open in 1930 when he was still an amateur. He was playing with Bobby Cruickshank that day. Byron and I became friends and worked many PGA schools together as teachers. We did the PGA school in San Antonio when a young fellow named Jack Nicklaus qualified for his PGA card.

Not many people know that Byron was named for the English poet Lord Byron—which I suppose is how Byron got that nickname in the press. Byron's grandmother was a fan of Lord Byron and named Byron's father John Byron Nelson. Byron, the golfer, is John Byron Nelson, Jr.

Byron has had his left hip replaced twice, but he has never let the pain keep him away from his love of playing golf. After the death of his beloved wife, Louise, he married a wonderful woman named Peggy. Byron and Peggy get out on the golf course a couple of times a week, he told me, and they have some pretty hot matches. Although Byron retired from tournament golf at a young age, having made his mark as a great champion, it has remained for him a game for a lifetime.

Who Is Talking Here?

WHEN I FIRST started doing lectures in front of my peers at PGA teaching seminars, I was very nervous. I began many of these sessions with the old story about the fellow whose neighbors decided he was so obnoxious that they would tar and feather him and ride him out of town on a rail. After they had smeared him with tar and layered him with feathers and boosted him onto the rail, he looked down at them and said, "To tell you the truth, if it weren't for the honor of this occasion, I would just as soon walk."

What I told my fellow pros was that if it weren't for the honor of being at the podium, I would just as soon—in fact, I would rather—be sitting in the audience, listening to someone else. I enjoyed listening to other teachers, because I already knew what I was going to say unless they taught me something that was new to me.

I felt awkward about using the pronoun "I." Jimmy Demaret followed me onto the stage once and told the crowd, "Do you realize we have been listening to this man for more than an hour, and he has never once said 'I'?"

This was a problem for me. I didn't like to say "I," but it's awfully hard to talk all day without doing it.

Today many celebrities, especially athletes, solve this "I" problem by referring to themselves in the third person, almost as if the athlete and the speaker were two different people. But this sounds rather silly to me, and, besides, if I had said, "Harvey Penick thinks you should do so-and-so," the other pros would have laughed me out of the room for being so pompous.

I wasn't the only teaching pro who worried about using "I" too much.

Eventually, some of the pros started saying "we," instead, when speaking of themselves as individuals. I decided this was a sign of modesty. I got to where I would actually say, "Please excuse us, we have to give a lesson." Or, "Next week, we will be away, as we are playing in a tournament in Fort Worth." It may have sounded like a prize fight manager telling his fighter, "Don't worry, they can't hurt us." But I went along, blissfully unaware of my misuse of this royal "we."

Then one day I read an article by Mark Twain. The famous humorist said, "There are only three kinds of people who have a right to say 'we' when they mean 'I.' The first is the head of a state or nation. The second is an editor. And the third is a person with a tapeworm."

After I read that, I went back to using "I."

Use a Tee

I BELIEVE YOU should always use a tee on a par-3 hole, simply because the tee gives you an advantage. I know there are many wonderful players, like Roberto De-Vicenzo, who just toss a ball onto the grass at a par-3 tee—and sometimes at a par 4—and go ahead and strike an excellent shot. But I still believe you should make use of the extra edge you get by using that little wooden peg.

One of my Texas team players refused to use a tee. This boy was a fine golfer who thought he didn't need a peg. He thought using a tee was a sign of inferiority, and he shrugged off my suggestions that he might be an even better player if he would use the tee as the rules allow.

Finally one day I remarked to him, "You know, Bobby Jones never used a tee when he was young."

"Is that right?" my boy said, as if at last I had justified him.

I said, "Yes. But when Jones became a great champion, he always used a tee."

My player changed his habit that very day.

One warning about using tees, though. You may want to tee the ball high on a par 4 when you will hit it with a driver on the upswing for maximum distance. But on a par 3, tee the ball low. All you are using the tee for is to give yourself a perfect lie.

I see too many high handicappers who tee the ball half an inch high to hit it with a medium iron on a par 3, and the result is usually a poor shot. A ball that is teed high might look easy to hit with an iron, but that is an illusion.

Charlie the Ballplayer

———

I HAVE OFTEN wished that Charlie Crenshaw, Jr., had been as serious about his golf as his younger brother, Ben. I think Charlie Jr. might have had as much championship potential as Ben.

When they were little boys, their father, Charlie, gave young Charlie Jr. a cut-off 6-iron and Ben, who was fifteen months the junior, a cut-off 7-iron. I put new grips on both clubs, and the boys set off to learn golf. Ben spent much more time on the putting green than his brother, going around and around the putting clock with his dad and with Wilmer Allison, the tennis champion, but from tee to green Charlie hit the ball about as well as Ben did. I think Charlie was a little longer and Ben was a little straighter.

By the time they reached high school, Charlie's interests veered more toward football and baseball than toward golf. I was afraid Ben, a natural athlete, might follow in Charlie's footsteps and start lifting weights and pumping up those muscles that are of no help on the golf course. To my great relief, Ben chose to stick with golf.

Charlie won a baseball scholarship to the University of

Texas, where he was a four-year letterman in the out-field. Charlie played in three College World Series, a considerable achievement. He played on the same team with Burt Hooton, who went on to become a star pitcher in the major leagues.

Charlie quit playing golf for a number of years, but I'm happy to say that he returned to the game and now carries a low handicap. He shot a 73 from the back tees at our Pete Dye course during a tournament, and that takes some talent.

Not long ago I mentioned to Charlie that I was sorry he hadn't concentrated on golf as a youngster.

Charlie laughed and said, "If you've got a brother who plays golf like Ben, it's not difficult to decide to change sports."

Brownie

AT OUR CLUB near Riverside Drive we had a dog named Brownie who hung out around the place and loved to ride around the course beside me in a golf cart. Most people at the club liked Brownie, but her admirers did not include our greens superintendent.

The reason for this was that Brownie was constantly at war with the ground squirrels who lived on the course. When Brownie spotted a ground squirrel, she would leap out of the cart, chase the squirrel into its tunnel and then begin at once to dig a big hole. The dirt would go flying out from Brownie's paws faster than a man could move it with a shovel.

Our greens superintendent kept asking that something be done about Brownie.

Billy Penn came up with the solution.

At a meeting of the board of directors, Penn brought up the motion and the vote was carried—making Brownie an honorary member of Austin Country Club.

For the Tall Player

THERE ARE SOME top golfers who are very tall people— George Archer, Andy North, Tom Weiskopf, young Ernie Els and others—but the average player who is much above six feet tall has always been considered to be at a disadvantage because at address he is so much farther from the ball.

The two things that I stress for tall pupils are balance and tempo.

Balance is important to any player, but especially so for the tall. There is a center of balance—some call it gravity—for the golf swing that is generally believed to be somewhere near the belly button. Shorter players are able to turn this center during their swing with much more ease than taller players, whose long legs and long arms often struggle trying to coordinate with their hips.

The tempo of a tall player's swing must be smooth and at a speed that allows good balance in the feet, knees and hips. Too fast a swing or any sudden movement in the swing can throw off the tall player's balance. Usually the tall player has a long swing that carries the clubhead fast enough that an effort to hit hard through the ball is not necessary.

The tall player must pay particular attention, too, to maintaining the same posture through the swing that was established at address. I see many tall pupils who can't resist the urge to dive toward the ball during the downswing and then suddenly bob upward, as if to correct this faulty movement.

Having clubs of the proper length can often correct this up-and-down move in the swing. But a tall player does not necessarily need longer clubs. The important measurement is from the hands to the ground, not from the top of the head to the ball. Sometimes short players with short arms need longer clubs than players who are a foot taller.

David Robinson, a pro basketball star who is more than seven feet tall, came to Golfsmith in Austin to have a set of clubs fitted to his requirements. Robinson snapped several shafts with his powerful swing during testing before the proper clubs were assembled for him—five inches above standard length.

The most important thing of all for a tall player is to learn to hit the ball solidly, which requires good balance and tempo. A long swing with good tempo and with solid contact will produce plenty of distance.

Tall players can look very graceful at golf. One of the most beautiful swings of all time is that of Tom Weiskopf, who is several inches over six feet. George Bayer, who is six feet five, in his younger days hit the ball as far as any man alive, and looked good doing it. I keep hearing a story—I even read it in a magazine—that I have been giving lessons to Michael Jordan, the basketball star, who is six feet six. I have never met Michael Jordan. Someone did phone the golf shop claiming to be him, but I doubt that it was. From this supposed call, the story began that Jordan had asked what I would charge for a lesson, and I replied, "Five dollars and you furnish your own shag balls."

If he ever does call, I'll just tell him to come on and see me, no fee attached. I've watched Jordan play golf on television, and I'd like to watch him on the practice range.

Thoughts on Taking Dead Aim

ONE NIGHT AT a dinner party I heard a university professor remark that a chicken is an egg's way of making another egg.

I'd never thought about it that way before, but I realized at once that he was right. The egg came first, of course. We all come from eggs. Nobody arrives on earth full grown.

While they went on conversing at the table, my thoughts drifted to golf, and I knew that what the professor had said could be applied to teaching.

Inside every golfer there is an egg that we may say is where your golf swing comes from.

If it is an egg with a powerful, positive picture that calls forth right behavior, it will produce good play.

If it is an egg with negative thoughts and flawed motions that call forth wrong behavior, it can be changed by an act of faith.

Taking Dead Aim is an act of faith.

Steve Reid, who used to play on the PGA Tour, told me he was playing at Prestwick in Scotland one summer. Steve had hit a long drive onto the left side of the fairway, but the green was hidden by mounds of tall grass and bushes.

His caddie told him, "See that white house in the distance? Well, best you aim at the lower bedroom window on the right."

Steve whacked a long iron boring through the wind, apparently the shot of a lifetime. Grinning, Steve turned to the caddie expecting to hear, "Well done."

The caddie said, "Boonker."

"Boonker?" Steve yelled. "What do you mean boonker? I hit a perfect shot, right where you told me."

The caddie said, "Nae, I said the lower bedroom window on the right. You were one window too far left. You're in the boonker."

Steve told me that he thought he took aim until he started thinking about Taking Dead Aim—as evinced by the lower bedroom window on the right—and, "I realized by comparison to what that caddie wanted, I had played on the tour for years thinking I was aiming when really I was just aiming at the whole wide world."

When I ask you to Take Dead Aim, I mean that for a few seconds you should become calm but aware, putting all your best attention to the moment at hand. You make what I think of as the sweet calculations of wind and weather and distance, and see a sharp picture of your ball striking your target in your mind. Bobby Fischer, the chess champion, said that when it was his turn to play, he considered only one move—the right one. You take out the club your mind tells your muscles is the right one to swing. At this point your imagination is stronger than your willpower. Your body will do what your mind tells it to do. You have no doubt, no fear. For those few seconds you are what you think.

That's Taking Dead Aim. Trust yourself.

A Bow to Jack O'Brien

PLAYERS ON ALL professional tours today owe their thanks to a San Antonio sportswriter named Jack O'Brien, who was a friend to golf. In the winter of 1921, O'Brien noticed that the winner of the U.S. Open had won five hundred dollars, while two prizefighters had been paid twenty-five thousand dollars each for trying to beat their brains out.

With a nudge from John Bredemus, the extraordinary athlete and golf architect, O'Brien conceived of a winter golf tour to start in Texas with decent purses for the time. He found backing from the Chamber of Commerce. They sold San Antonio as "the City Where the Sun Goes For The Winter." O'Brien sought out Gene Sarazen and asked if he thought the top players would show up to play for five thousand dollars in prizes. "For that money, we'll play in a pasture," Gene told him.

The first Texas Open was played at San Antonio's Brackenridge Park in the winter of 1922, when I was eighteen and about to become head pro. Brackenridge

Park used rubber mats on the tees. Bob MacDonald won that first tournament. The Texas Open has been played nearly every year since, and from O'Brien's tournament grew the professional tours as we know them today.

Jack was a friend of us pros and a good golfing companion. I salute his memory and his spirit.

Talking to Terry

I'M SURE TERRY Dill will take it as a compliment when I say he always has marched to the sound of his own drummer. Terry is a long-hitting Senior Tour player now, and a lawyer as well as being a golf course designer and an expert in a number of subjects. When he played on my golf team, Terry liked to do things his own way. That was fine with me.

I was careful what I said to Terry if I was trying to persuade him to accept a suggestion.

One afternoon my golf team was out on the course playing practice rounds in a very hard wind. I liked for them to play in the wind, so they would learn to handle it. But I looked up from whatever I was doing in the golf shop and saw Terry walking in with his bag over his shoulder after only nine holes.

"What's the matter, Terry?" I asked.

"It's too windy," he said.

I nodded. "Well, I learn something every day. Until now, I thought the wind only bothered butterflies."

Terry looked at me for a moment, picked up his bag and returned to play the back nine.

The Bullfighter

MARCELINO MORENO PLAYED on the Texas A&M golf team in the middle 1950s with Bobby Nichols and some other long hitters. Marcelino was slight of stature and could nowhere near keep up with his teammates off the tee, but he had a wonderful short game and could get up and down like a magician.

Marcelino came to me and asked what he could do to take his game up a notch. I told him the only thing I could see was that he needed more distance. Marcelino applied himself diligently on the practice tee and eventually picked up quite a few yards in length—but he lost his touch around the greens.

In 1957 the NCAA tournament was held at Broadmoor in Colorado Springs. By this time, Marcelino could wallop his drive out there pretty well, but his short game was such a mess that he was putting with his sand wedge.

Somehow, Marcelino qualified in the top sixty-four and made it into match play, where he was eventually beaten by Rex Baxter. How Marcelino got that far putting with a sand wedge on those tricky Broadmoor greens has always been to me one of the more amazing stories in golf.

After college, Marcelino went to Mexico City, where

he became a bullfighter and a greens superintendent at the same time. Marcelino would supervise the greens at two country clubs during the week, and then on weekends he would fly off to fight the bulls. I doubt if there has ever been another such combination.

Just an Inch or So

ONE OF THE briefest lessons I ever gave was to Eldridge Miles, who is director of golf at Gleneagles Country Club in Plano, north of Dallas. Eldridge is a good player, so I didn't expect to have much to do when I heard he was waiting on me at the practice range, but this was even easier than I had thought.

When I drove up to him and got out of my golf cart, Eldridge was hitting his 3-iron. I walked over to him and with my cane I moved his ball back about an inch or so in his stance.

Eldridge glanced at me and with his clubhead returned the ball to where he had been playing it.

I reached out with my cane and moved the ball back again, just an inch or so.

Once more Eldridge nudged the ball forward with his clubhead.

Again I tapped the ball with my cane and moved it back an inch or so.

I guess Eldridge decided to humor me. He left the ball where I had moved it and swung his 3-iron and smacked it long and high, as good a 3-iron as I ever saw.

I got back in my cart and drove away.

Later one of my members, who had been hitting balls nearby, told me Eldridge had hit a few more perfect 3-irons and then had asked, "Where did he go?"

"I don't know," my member said.

"When's he coming back?" Eldridge asked.

"I doubt if he's coming back," my member said. "I think your lesson is over."

Eldridge sought me out in the shade of the live oak trees where I frequently pass the time.

"I'm hitting it great," he said.

"No reason why you shouldn't hit it great all the time," I said.

"How much do I owe you?" he asked.

I said, "You're a fellow pro. You don't owe me a thing."

Sonny Rhodes told me he played golf with Eldridge recently and saw some wonderful long iron shots. I must say I'm not surprised. Eldridge had been only an inch or so away from almost perfect.

Born in Scotland

THE AUSTIN COUNTRY Club was born in Scotland, I like to think.

Lewis Hancock, one of our most prominent citizens, used to take a yearly holiday in Europe. In 1897, he fell in love with the game of golf in Scotland. Soon as he returned to Austin, he gathered his friends Bob Connerly, T. W. Gregory and T. B. Cochran. They agreed that in order to keep fit a businessman needed relaxation and exercise, as well as sunshine and fresh air—and golf supplied those things.

They laid out nine holes on farm land in north Austin, had sand greens built, and began playing golf. Hancock, Connerly, Gregory and Cochran were the first foursome in Austin history. They hung their coats on tree branches and started playing. No locker room, no showers, not even a shed for a clubhouse. They were soon joined by George Rotan and a total of sixteen charter members. Rotan played on the first Walker Cup team.

Bob Connerly won the state championship five times, as did Rotan.

In those early days they used wire mesh instead of bunkers. A ball that landed in the wire mesh could be dropped out one club length.

They built a clubhouse for one hundred dollars. A few years later, they built a large, beautiful frame clubhouse on the east side of Waller Creek. I was head pro in that clubhouse until 1934, when fire destroyed it in the middle of the night. Using brick and stone from the old Main Building of the University of Texas, we rebuilt the clubhouse promptly, even though it was during the Great Depression and money was scarce.

Not only is Austin Country Club one of the oldest in this country, it is one of the first to take women's golf seriously.

Among my mementos I have a copy of an announcement of a women's match at the club on Washington's Birthday in 1900, four years before I was born and six years before the organization of the Texas Golf Association.

The announcement includes a warning to men: "During competition no players will be allowed on the course other than the women competitors."

Memorial Park

MY OLD FRIEND John Bredemus in 1936 built two of the best golf courses in the United States—Colonial Country Club in Fort Worth, and Memorial Park in Houston. Most golfers have heard of Colonial, which has hosted the U.S. Open and was the home course for Ben Hogan. But few outside Houston know of Memorial Park, a municipal course that was every bit as good as Colonial until Memorial began to fall into decay after years of neglect and hundreds of thousands of rounds of golf.

I am happy to say that Memorial Park is being restored to the original Bredemus design by Dave Marr and Jay and Bernie Riviere. Memorial is practically in downtown Houston, yet is a beautiful, pastoral setting with tall trees and is circled by a jogging path that Bredemus insisted on putting there, rather than the road through the course that some of the city planners wanted. In my opinion, it is quite a coup for Houston to have this championship course for the public.

Bredemus was a quiet man who traveled with a bag of books, a few golf clubs and a sack of checkers and a checker board. He had been a star athlete at both Dartmouth and Princeton and was the AAU All-Around champion in track and field before he started playing golf in 1914 at Van Cortlandt Park in New York City, the first public course in the country. John would never set foot inside a country club, even though he built plenty of country club courses. I don't know why. We became close and I invited him into Austin Country Club, but John would only say, "I don't belong inside." John would visit the Burkes at River Oaks and sit under the trees and play checkers with the members, but he would never enter the clubhouse door.

While he was building Memorial Park, the project kept running out of money. One day John went to see Jesse Jones, the tycoon who had a large say in how government funds were spent for public works during the Depression.

John left his muddy shoes in the hall and entered Jones's office barefoot so as not to put tracks on the oriental carpets. Jones was impressed by this and gave John the money he needed to finish Memorial Park. Afterward, John was known as "Barefoot John."

Bernie Riviere, who played for me at the University of Texas and won the amateur championship of Colombia, South America, before he turned pro, told me that when Jay and David went to work at rebuilding Memorial, they decided the half-dozen ponds on the course needed to be dug out. The ponds had silted up to six inches deep. Marr and the Rivieres had the ponds dug to a depth of eight feet—and found a world of golf balls, many more than fifty years old.

The mark of a Bredemus course is that it is terribly difficult for expert players but a pleasant experience for dubs. This is certainly true of the seventy-two-hundred-yard Memorial Park, where I would like to think a major championship will be held one of these years.

Wild Bill

BILL MORETTI, WHO runs the teaching academy at the Hills on Lake Travis in the western outskirts of Austin, played college golf at Florida International University in Miami, where one of his teachers was my old friend Bill Mehlhorn at the Fontainebleau golf course.

In his prime, Mehlhorn struck the ball as purely as anyone ever has. Even Ben Hogan used to love to watch Mehlhorn play. If he hadn't been such an awful putter, Wild Bill Mehlhorn (he was given that nickname by his pal Leo Diegel, who used to write newspaper articles as well as play championship golf) would have been the favorite to win every tournament he entered. Wild Bill won more than twenty pro tournaments as it was.

Mehlhorn had the worst case of yips I have ever seen. Playing in a pro-pro team event at the Biltmore in Miami one year, Bill shot a 34 on the front and opened the back side with two birdies. He was ten feet from the cup on the next hole and told his partner, Earl Holland, to pick up his ball because Bill wouldn't need him. Then Bill took six putts, the last five from within two feet. We played in a tournament in Dallas, where Bill had about a four-footer to tie for the lead late in the final round. Craig Wood was standing in the fringe on the back of the green and had to hop into the air to avoid being hit by Bill's putt after it sped past the hole. Hogan said he was playing in a tournament with Mehlhorn when Bill hit his second shot two feet from the hole and then had to play his fourth from a bunker.

Moretti told me he played golf with Mehlhorn quite often in Miami, and I asked if Wild Bill had ever solved his putting woes. "I don't think so," Moretti told me. "Usually he'd hit his approach shot to the green and then go get into his golf cart without bothering to putt at all."

Baseball was Mehlhorn's favorite game, and he taught that the golf swing and the swing with a baseball bat are very similar, as is the golf swing to the act of throwing a baseball underhanded and sort of sidearmed.

There's one thing about Mehlhorn that I wish golfers everywhere would copy. Wild Bill played fast. He and Jock Hutchison played a thirty-six-hole exhibition at the Old Course at St. Andrews during the 1920s in three hours. The gallery had to run to keep up with them. In those days we didn't dawdle on the golf course, even during tournaments. When Harry Cooper won the Los Angeles Open in 1926, he and George Von Elm played the last round in two and a half hours in front of a big gallery.

I remember what Mehlhorn used to say at every teaching seminar. He would say the secret to the golf swing is muscles and joints at ease in their movement. Just as I do, Bill was always telling pupils to relax their elbows, since the elbow is the most important joint we have in the movement of the golf swing. Bill and I were in total agreement that the attempt to keep a straight left arm means ruination for most golfers.

Horton and Lema

HORTON SMITH, ONE of the best putters of all time, told me the method he used to teach putting to young Tony Lema.

Horton would have Lema put his own left hand on his left thigh at address and then make an ideal stroke with his right hand and arm. Once this right-handed stroke felt correct, Tony would place his left hand on the handle along with the right and copy the stroke.

I think this is an excellent system. In putting, you must have a system you can rely on, and Horton's is as good as I ever heard of.

Horton and Grace

ONE OF OUR best Texas amateurs is a man from Fort Worth named John Grace. Besides winning our state championship and many other titles, John was runner-up in the U.S. Amateur to Jerry Pate, who won the U.S. Open two years later.

As a boy at the Country Club of Detroit, John learned

golf from Horton Smith, who recommended that John come see me if he had any problems after moving to Texas, because Horton and I were old friends and taught very much alike.

Horton insisted that John practice his short game 90 percent of the time and spend only 10 percent refining his long shots. "Your short game will help your long game in every way, but your long game won't help your short game at all," Horton told him. My pupils have heard me say the same thing many times.

Unless he is entered in a tournament, John plays golf about once a week at Shady Oaks in Fort Worth. But he practices his short game every afternoon, and every night at home John practices putting on the carpet.

His wife, Phoebe, told me, "I have a rule—no pitch shots in the house. But I find a golf ball in a flower pot now and then. Of course, John always claims to know nothing about it."

The "I" in Maxfli

EVER SINCE HE was new to teaching a number of years ago, Mark Steinbauer has showed up regularly to visit with me on the practice range at Austin Country Club or at home or during my spells in the hospital. I have always enjoyed talking with Mark. It has been a pleasure to watch him progress to where he is now director of golf for the big resort called The Woodlands in the pines near Houston.

On his most recent visit, Mark was discussing one type of person who can be a test of the teacher's patience. This is the person who always wants to know "why?" Mark calls them "analytical." I call them doctors, lawyers, accountants and engineers, for the most part.

I remembered a judge who showed up one day for a lesson at the old club on Riverside Drive. It was in the shag ball days, and the judge brought a fat sack of balls with him. Everything I said to the judge, he would peer at me and frown and ask, "Why should I do that? Where does that fit in my total swing?"

Finally I said, "Judge, I'm going to tell you the real secret of golf."

I picked up one of his shag balls and showed it to him.

"See where it says Maxfli?" I said. "I want you to keep your eye on the 'i' in Maxfli. Think about that and that alone. The reason, as you can see, makes good sense. Walter Hagen always said that even as great a player as he needed to look at the ball when he hit it."

The judge began to hit the ball solidly almost at once and went away believing he knew the secret of golf. As long as this teaching got results for the judge, it truly was the secret of golf.

As I told Mark, keeping your eye on the ball is a teaching that will do no harm and may even be of great benefit, as it was to the judge. By keeping his eye on the "i" in Maxfli, he had something definite to concentrate on and could more easily exclude the many questions that rambled through his analytical mind.

A teacher must beware of what is said to a pupil. What the teacher says is the strongest thought in the pupil's mind and cannot be easily retracted.

Bob Watson

SHORTLY AFTER THE end of World War II, a big, good-looking fellow named Bob Watson was discharged from the Air Force and came to the University of Texas on the GI Bill. Bob set out to try to make our golf team and won our qualifying tournament to become the number-one man in his first year on campus. This was despite his West Texas grip, a four-knuckle hold on the club that produced a big hook. I wanted Bob to change his grip, but I didn't want to force him into it. The best way to make a change is to put into the pupil's mind a picture that will show the pupil what you are talking about more vividly and permanently than words could ever convey.

There was a fine golfer named Morris Norton in Bob's hometown of Wichita Falls. One day I said, "Bob, do you know Morris Norton?" He said yes. I said, "Morris Norton's hands look better on the club than almost anyone I have ever seen. Do you think you could place your hands on the club just like he does?"

Bob said he thought he could, and before long he was doing it. Bob won the Southwest Conference championship two years in a row. He was one of my favorite players in my long career as a coach.

After graduation, Bob went to work as a club pro in the New York area and became one of the best in the business as well as a superb teacher. I sent him a number of my Texas boys to be his assistants over the years. Bob remained a good player, too. He won the Metropolitan

Open and the Westchester Open. In the winter he would head south and win tournaments like the Panama Open. I remember that in the Jamaica Open, Bob thought he had first-place money cinched until Roberto DeVicenzo knocked in a double-eagle deuce at the end to edge him out.

In 1959, Bob and I walked the course at Winged Foot and talked golf all through the U.S. Open, which Billy Casper won that year. Bob called me a "brain picker" because I asked him so many questions. So I asked him one more. I asked, "Can I see your grip?" He grinned and placed his hands on the club—just like Morris Norton. Bob never forgot.

The Masters Champion

IT WAS A joyful drive to the airport with Helen in the spring of 1984. We were joining a group welcoming Ben Crenshaw back to Austin. In his bag he would be carrying the green jacket of a Masters champion. Ben had finished second in the Masters in 1983, but yesterday he had won it, one of the grandest prizes in golf.

Ben had been off his game for a while. He had a health problem, and there was a lot on his mind. I watched him play golf on television, and I wanted to visit with him. I started praying every night that Ben would come see me.

So of course he did come see me shortly before the

Masters. We looked at his swing and checked his ball position, address and clubface angle to see that they remained as they had always been. We talked about achieving a calm mind. I believe if you have the desire to win and you let God's hand rest on your shoulder, if it is your turn to win, you will win.

"Just swing like Ben," I told him. I felt good about Ben when he left for the tournament. Ben led the first day at the Masters, and Tommy Kite took the lead by the end of the third round. Ben got the lead again on the tenth hole of the final day by sinking a sixty-foot birdie putt, his third birdie in a row. I was sad for Tommy, but I cried tears of happiness in front of my TV when Ben became the Masters champion, just as I did eight years later when Tommy won the U.S. Open at Pebble Beach. Tommy and Ben are like sons to me.

At the 1984 Masters, Ben showed he had faith in his own natural way. He trusted himself. That's what I was thinking about as Helen and I drove to the airport, and I couldn't wait to see Ben wearing that new green jacket.

Helen

THE MOST FORTUNATE day of my life was the Sunday morning I decided to go with my mother to the Hyde Park Christian Church, where she was a charter member. We sat in the back row that morning, but my eyes were drawn to a beautiful girl who was singing in the choir. I kept staring at her, hoping she would look back at me. After the service, I asked about her and found out her name was Helen Holmes. She was the daughter of a preacher who had moved from town to town, building a church wherever he went.

Helen had a teacher's certificate from Southwest Texas State in San Marcos. She had moved to Austin to attend the University of Texas and to teach school. I found out where she lived and made plans to become acquainted with her. One day I dressed in my finest coat and tie and cap, wearing my new knickers, and borrowed my brother Tom's car. I pulled up near Helen as she was walking along the sidewalk and asked if I might give her a ride to school.

She said, "No."

A few days later I contrived to be where Helen was crossing the street. I introduced myself again and asked if she might allow me to phone her sometime. She said that would be okay. I waited fifteen minutes and called her and asked her to go with me to the Texas Open in San Antonio for a day.

Helen didn't know what a golf pro was, but she had never been to San Antonio and agreed to accompany me. When I went by to pick her up, she was the most gorgeous girl I have ever seen. The only thing wrong was she was wearing high heels. I worked up the courage to explain to her that she would have to change shoes, and we set off on the drive to San Antonio.

When we arrived at Brackenridge Park, Bob Hope and Bing Crosby were getting ready to tee off. Helen was excited. Seeing Hope and Crosby might have been what convinced her that golf must be a good game.

I knew Helen was the woman I wanted to spend my life with, but I was afraid her father might not let her marry a golf pro. Reverend Holmes was a good athlete and a fan of baseball and football. He told me golf looked like a simple thing. I took him to the club and gave him a lesson. He tried and tried, but he couldn't hit the ball. Finally he threw down the club and shouted, "Confound it!" That was the strongest language he ever used.

Within a year Helen and I got married. We lived in a lovely home on Laurel Lane in Hyde Park, not far from the club. The President of the University lived down the street from us. Our daughter, Kathryn Lee, was born, and a few years later Helen became pregnant with our son, Tinsley. We needed another bedroom. The house directly behind us came up for sale, and we bought it. There was a huge oak tree in the front yard, locally famous as the "lying down oak" because it lay along the ground before it gently began to rise. Old timers told us Indians had bent that tree as a sapling and tied it down to point north. Tinsley's dog would hop onto the trunk and scamper up into the highest branches, the only dog I ever saw climb a tree.

Helen would always follow me when I played in a tournament. Critical remarks from the spectators would annoy her. One day after I had missed a short putt, I heard someone in the gallery say, "Why couldn't he make that one?" Then I heard Helen say, "If you think you can do any better, why don't you get out there and try it?"

In 1950 Austin Country Club moved from Hancock Park to a new location on the southeast edge of town near the Colorado River. Helen and I bought some land near the club, and she designed her dream home, which we built near the twelfth tee. Helen wanted to name our dirt road Tinlee Drive—after Kathryn Lee and Tinsley—but one morning the city came out and put up a sign naming it Penick Drive. We lived in that house for thirty-two years.

My brother, Tom, and I owned a driving range on land we bought where the Municipal Auditorium is now on the bank of the river. It was the only driving range in town and one of the few in Texas. Seven days a week, I would go to the club early in the morning and unlock the doors and stay until lock-up time in the evening. Then I would pick up Helen and we would go to the driving range. The long hours were hard on both of us, and eventually Tom and I shut down the driving range.

My senior year in high school, while I was working in the golf shop, an influential member of the club had offered to get me an appointment to West Point. I told him, "No, thank you, sir. The only thing in life I want to be is a golf pro." I never regretted that decision, but later I did wonder if it was fair to Helen to be the wife of a club pro who was seldom at home. Helen, bless her soul, put up with me. I could not have lasted so long in this job without her love and support.

In 1972 I was driving too fast in a golf cart, heading for the barn where I heard vandals were wrecking the place, and I hit a bump and fell out and broke my back. Of all the ways for me to get hurt! I was always opposed to golf carts, and now one of them had almost killed me. Every day and night for the rest of my life, I have been in pain. Helen takes care of me.

As my brother, Tom, had taught me, life was not created for the sole purpose of making me comfortable. I learned it was better to meet the pain head on and go about my business than to try to hide from it behind pills and self-pity. But without Helen, I might have given up.

When our new Pete Dye course opened on the north-west side of town, Helen and I moved again. By now Tinsley was the head pro. I was called the head pro emeritus, which in fact meant I was the starter at the first tee. I used to laugh and say, "In only sixty years I have managed to work my way into the worst job at the club."

And all this time, through all the long hours and the sickness, Helen has stood by me and given me strength. She is the most wonderful, courageous person I have ever known. I thank God for sending me to the Hyde Park Christian Church that day so long ago, and I thank Helen for sharing her life with me.

Any time a young pro has asked me what is the most important thing to learn, I always say, "The most important thing, if you are lucky enough, is to marry the right person."

I did. I love you, Helen.

Epilogue

During the week of the 1995 Ryder Cup in Rochester, New York, there was an event held to honor Harvey Penick. Many of golf's top teachers were on the program. The keynote speaker was Tinsley Penick, Harvey's son, who more than twenty-five years earlier had replaced his father as head pro at Austin Country Club.

This is what Tinsley said.

GOOD EVENING. I'd like to thank Dan Parks for honoring my father here tonight and for staging this wonderful event. I'm flattered to be on the same program with these great teachers. These are some of the greatest names in golf in the latter part of the twentieth century. For me to appear with them is a great tribute to my father.

A friend of mine named Dick Harmon is the pro at River Oaks Country Club in Houston. One of his brothers, Craig, is the pro here at Oak Hill. They are sons of Claude Harmon, and they learned golf and teaching golf from their father. Dick says he thinks his father could start a sentence, and Dick could finish it.

I could say that about my father and myself. If my dad was right when he said he saw more golf shots than any man alive, then I've probably heard about more golf shots than any man alive.

Anyone who has been able to compare my father's teaching methods to those of the rest of the gentlemen on this program will probably notice a difference in approach.

My father's techniques might seem at odds with to-day's methods.

They're not high tech at all. They're very simple, sometimes frustratingly so.

Many people who took lessons from him wondered afterward what had happened.

Claude Harmon used to say about him, "It takes a lot of courage to teach like Harvey, to say as little as he does."

In fact, that was a deliberate part of my father's technique.

He reinforced a positive mental game, but did it in very subtle ways.

I think one of the reasons he is considered a great instructor is that he gave pupils confidence.

Dr. Tom Kirksey, an Austin cardiologist, took a lesson and later tried to figure out what Harvey had told him.

Dr. Kirksey shook his head, couldn't figure it out. But whatever it was, it worked. Dr. Kirksey later said that a lesson from my father was sort of like reading the Old Testament—there's an important message there, but you're not sure what it is.

Many teaching pros will prefer giving a lesson to a high handicapper over a scratch player. It's much easier to help a beginner, and any advice you give a very good player runs the risk of having a negative effect. My father was very conscious of that. But he had his own way of teaching the good players.

For example, Hal Underwood, who had a tremendous career as an amateur and was on the tour for a few years in the early '70s, once took a lesson from my father. Hal hit a lot of balls for about half an hour on the practice tee with my dad watching him closely but not saying a word. Finally, when there were no more balls to hit, Hal asked my father, "Well, what do you think?" My dad stood there another minute or so and finally said, "I don't know. Let me think about it overnight." And he turned around and walked off. The next day, my dad saw Hal at the club and said, "I've thought about it all night, and I don't recommend any change." Years later Hal is still amazed by the experience.

Few pros would dream of teaching like this. And most players today probably would demand more information. My father was famous for not changing anything about the golfer's swing, but not telling the golfer why.

My father inherited this technique from the methods of the old Scottish professionals who pretty much were the only instructors around in the early part of this century. Maybe the most famous of them was Stewart Maiden, who was Bobby Jones's instructor. There's a famous story about how Bobby was getting ready to play a tournament at Winged Foot and called Stewart in

Augusta and asked him to come up and look at his swing. Stewart took the train to New York and met up with Bobby on the practice tee. He watched Bobby take a couple of swings and said, "You don't hit the ball with your backswing, laddie." Then Stewart walked off.

One of the better instructors in the Austin area, Chuck Cook, decided to take on a personal challenge once and try to teach like my father for one week. His first lesson was with Omar Uresti, who at the time was playing for the University of Texas team and is now on the tour. Chuck made a suggestion about Omar's grip, and didn't say anything about what the objective was. Omar asked him, "Why would you want me to do that?" Chuck tried to do what my father would have done and said, "Don't think about it, just do it." But Omar kept asking, and after a short while Chuck threw up his hands and went back to his usual way of teaching.

I'd like to think my father's techniques are timeless. For the most part, he was self-taught as an instructor. It's important to remember that my father was already cad-dying at Austin Country Club when Francis Ouimet won the U.S. Open in 1913. My dad talked about the time William Howard Taft played the course and the Secret Service escorted the President around on horseback with their rifles. After my father became the pro in 1923, he was about the only recognized teaching pro in Texas for many years who was born in the United States.

My father did have some role models and some pros whose methods he greatly respected in his earlier years—especially Jack Burke, Sr., Bobby Jones, J. Victor East, who was also a club designer at Spalding, and Stewart Maiden.

In my opinion my father's greatest attribute was one that all great teachers have—complete confidence in himself. In his own mind he was absolutely sure he knew what was wrong with a golfer's swing. And that probably explains why his advice was so minimal much of the time—he wouldn't change a swing unless he was dead sure what the problem was.

The Little Red Book has a story about a lesson my father gave Don January to see if he was ready to join the tour. My father told him, "Don, some people are going to tell you that you're losing control at the top. Don't listen to them. Pack your bags and go to California and join the tour."

Sometimes his only advice would be something that would help the good player's frame of mind. He told Tom Kite when he joined the tour to go to dinner with good putters, the idea being that their confidence would be contagious. If you surround yourself with good, positive people, it will rub off on your game—and he applied that to other facets of life as well.

When Lanny Wadkins was at Austin Country Club earlier this year, my father told him that at one time he believed the turn in the golf swing was simply a way for the big muscles to get out of the way so the golfer could use the small muscles. Later on, after he had watched a lot of the modern pros on television, my dad decided it is best to use both the big and small muscles, as long as it is in the proper manner.

In fact, my father realized that many very successful players and instructors today have learned how to incorporate the whole body into the golf swing, and he accepted that. A swing like John Daly's would break many instructors' fundamentals. But my dad watched John on TV many times and would say, "I admire him because he found a swing that suits him. I'd advise him not to change it."

Seventy years as an instructor gave my dad a lot of experience to draw on. One day a vendor came to the club peddling a high-tech video machine. The salesman photographed my swing and printed it out in a series of sequence shots. I showed the prints to my dad.

He said, "That is really a high follow-through. How well did you hit it?"

I said, "I hit it good."

My dad said, "Horton Smith used to finish that high."

I think he was telling me a high finish is good if it works for me, but he had to go back fifty years to recall another finish as high as mine.

My father never bad-mouthed another instructor's methods. If a player was putting crosshanded, he might disagree but he would never say, "That's the stupidest putting stroke I ever saw." Instead, he would say, "It works for Bernhard Langer, but it might not work for you."

My father generally favored a strong grip. When Jack Nicklaus popularized the neutral grip, my father would say, "It works for Jack Nicklaus, but it might not work for most of us."

One of the fundamentals he taught was to position your eyes over the ball at address when putting. But when we were filming *The Little Green Video*, he decided he couldn't use that tip. Ben Crenshaw was doing the demonstration, and when Ben sets up, his eyes are not over the ball.

By the way, the filming of *The Little Green Video* was the first time that my father ever allowed Tom Kite to watch him give a lesson to Ben Crenshaw, or vice-versa. He understood how different the two players are, and he was concerned that a tip intended for one could subconsciously have a bad effect on the other.

A footnote about lifting the left heel on the backswing. My dad's preference was for the left heel to come off the ground. He gave Kathy Whitworth many, many lessons over the years. When Kathy was young, she used to drive to Austin from her home in New Mexico—at least a ten-hour drive—three or four times a month. She went on to make the LPGA Hall of Fame, and during her entire career she has never once lifted her left heel off the ground during the backswing, and my father never once said a word about it to her.

Before I close, here are just a few more examples of my father's teaching techniques. My father did not like for a pupil to warm up before a lesson. If they were hitting good, it could only get worse. If they were hitting bad, they would already have negative thoughts. My dad wanted to start fresh. My dad told his pupils to avoid weightlifting unless they were being instructed by someone who was qualified and who understood the golf swing. He also told people it wasn't a good idea to go swimming before playing golf.

On alignment, my father was more concerned with the player hitting the ball solid. He would say, "Don't worry about alignment until you start hitting solid. Then I'll tell you where to line up." He would remind pupils that Lee Trevino and Sam Snead line up thirty yards apart, Lee to play his fade and Sam to play his draw.

My father coached the University of Texas golf team for thirty-three years. He not only taught a lot of good young golfers, he also learned from them. He would always ask a new player about the methods and teaching techniques of his local pro. My dad gained a lot of knowledge from these experiences.

My dad always said that the day he stopped learning would be the day he stopped teaching. He must have been learning right up to the day he died, because he never stopped teaching. You may have heard the story about Ben Crenshaw visiting my father in his bedroom a few days before he was to leave for Augusta this year. Ben told my father he was having a little trouble with putting.

My dad asked Ben, "Have you been taking a couple of practice strokes before each putt and imagining the ball going into the hole?"

Ben said, "You know, I don't think I have been."

My father said, "Get a putter and let me watch you take a few strokes on the carpet."

The lesson went on for about an hour.

Two weeks later, Ben won the Masters.

So if the question is, "Would Harvey Penick's methods work today?" I guess the answer is "Yes, they do."

Thank you all very much for the honor of being able to share a few memories with you.